MW00388155

BULL RUN

First victory for the South

or the battle of Manassas

21 July 1861

by Pascal Le Pautremat

Translated from the French by Alan McKAY

*Cartography and schemes Jean-Marie Mongin, 3D map by Grégory Proch
uniformological plates by André Jouineau, color plates by Ludovic Letrun*

Histoire & Collections

4 (colour plate by Ludovic Letrun, © Histoire & Collections 2010)

Colonel Alfred Duffie of the 1st Rhode Island, Union Cavalry. Even if this picture was probably taken in 1862 before the second Battle of the Bull Run, the Volunteer Cavalry officers had the same look about them in July 1861. (RR)

CONTENTS

B
ULL RUN FOR THE NORTH, MANASSAS FOR THE SOUTH; the difference in the name given to the same battle is because the Southerners chose to give full-scale battles the name of the nearest town, in this case Manassas. The Northerners associated the geographic features of the battle areas to the battles, hence the name taken from the river Bull Run; nothing really destined this little river in Virginia bearing the same name to leave its mark on history in such a tragic way: the American people's collective memory has retained this name because it is synonymous with one of the first big battles of the Civil War.

Above.
The Union camp on the eve of the so-called Battle of the Bull Run. The army defending Washington with its impeccable regulation turn out was quickly given a hiding, and for some people the fun and picnic very quickly turned out to be a nightmare.
(RR)

The Battle of Bull Run took place in July 1861 and although its overall impact was in fact rather limited, its influence on the Civil War itself was considerable. Its psychological effect was undeniable, particularly for the Northerners who became aware of the realities of war and the challenges that they had to face up to. Besides, the first battle of Manassas was special since it was the first sizeable engagement that involved troops brought in by train and in this case it enabled the Confederates to win the battle.

The Battle of Bull Run – Manassas was particularly important for United States military history. Firstly, because it recalled the fratricidal conflict that bathed the United States in blood between 1861 and 1865. The Civil War was responsible for some 620 000 deaths of which some 360 000 were on the Union side when the overall population of the United States was 32 million in 1860, nine million of which were in the southern states. Secondly becau-

se the Johnny Rebs or Rebels, the pejorative nickname given to the Southern soldiers by the Union, in their July 1861 momentum were never so near reaching Washington, a situation which they subsequently tried to repeat, in vain, with the last attempt being made during the Battle of Gettysburg (1-3 July 1863) and a later hit-and-run raid doomed to failure in July 1864.

Facing them were the *Billy Yanks* or Yankees – the disdainful nickname given the Union soldiers by the Southerners – who in this particular case lacked daring and conviction, and were no doubt over-confident, circumstances compounded by the presence near the battlefield of Congressmen, members of the gentry, who had come down to watch the show. For the Unionists the epilogue to the Battle of Manassas was very far from being among the most heroic since it resulted in a frantic flight in indescribable chaos, a jumble of maddened soldiers and terrorised civilians. And even if in the end the North won the Civil

War it had a lot of difficulty in its struggle against Confederate opposition when this consisted of harassment and guerrilla tactics taking clever advantage of nature, the valleys and the large forest areas in West Virginia.

All that being said and done, the Battle of Bull Run-Manassas, a fight between masses of amateurs led by professional officers, testified to the existence of two existing, culturally opposed communities who confronted each other to defend their convictions.

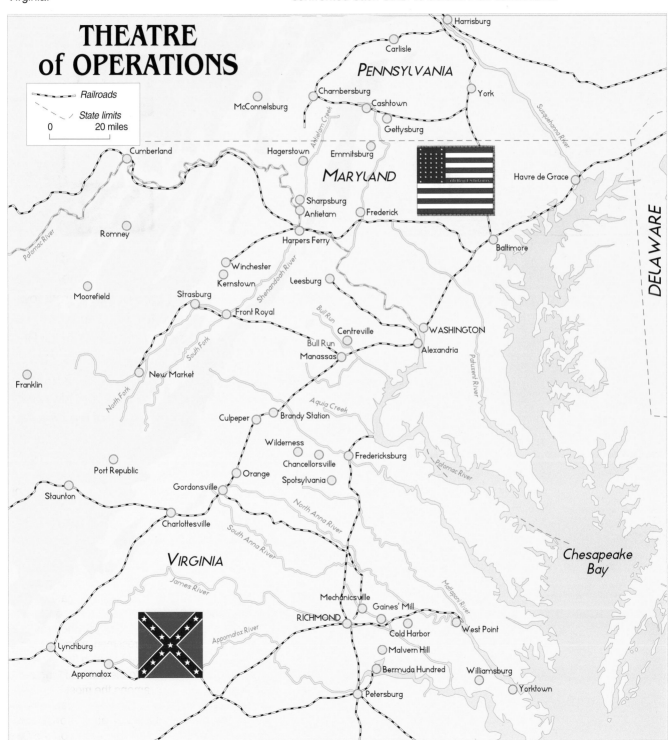

THEATRE of OPERATIONS

Railroads

State limits

0   20 miles

PENNSYLVANIA

Harrisburg

Carlisle

Chambersburg

Cashtown

York

McConnelsburg

Gettysburg

Susquehanna River

Cumberland

Hagerstown

Emmitsburg

Antietam Creek

MARYLAND

Havre de Grace

DELAWARE

Romney

Sharpsburg

Antietam

Frederick

Potomac River

Harpers Ferry

Baltimore

Winchester

Moorefield

Kernstown

Shenandoah River

Leesburg

Strasburg

Front Royal

South Fork

Bull Run

Centreville

WASHINGTON

New Market

Bull Run

Manassas

Alexandria

Patuxent River

North Fork

Franklin

Aquia Creek

Culpeper

Brandy Station

Potomac River

Wilderness

Port Republic

Chancellorsville

Fredericksburg

Orange

Spotsylvania

Gordonsville

Staunton

North Anna River

Chesapeake Bay

Charlottesville

South Anna River

VIRGINIA

James River

Mechanicsville

Gaines' Mill

RICHMOND

Mattaponi River

Lynchburg

Appomatox River

Cold Harbor

West Point

Malvern Hill

Appomatox

Bermuda Hundred

Williamsburg

Petersburg

Yorktown

1861, THE BUILD

WHEN THE UNION AND CONFEDERATE STATES MOBILISED, both sides were convinced their cause was legitimate. The Northern states had an extremely strong industrial base, widely supported by the population of the North-East Coast. On the contrary, the Southern states were mainly agricultural, influenced by a plantation society where conservative and traditional convictions tended to reject any Unionist development put into effect by Washington. The Southerners feared above all losing their socio-economic bases, their very identity

A COUNTRY OF DISSENSIONS SPLITS UP

After Fort Sumter fell on 12 April 1861 – the starting point of the war with as background a plan to secede from the Union which quickly spread among the Southern states – the belligerents let themselves get carried away by war fever and a communicative obstinacy to defend their own cause, naturally thought to be fair and legitimate. Each side put forward the notions of ancestry, traditions and convictions which had to be preserved, with the Northern combatants and the population as a whole of the Union states being very much attached to the Constitution.

All the Americans, no matter what their choice, were convinced of the need to invest themselves, to defend their values, amalgamating duty, faith and posterity in the name of their children. Jefferson Davis (1808-1889) himself put forward "the sacred right to self-government" by adopting the principle dear to the Founding Fathers of the American nation. Moreover the South was convinced that the Unionists were planning to conquer their territory to get their hands on all their goods and property, and destroy their society. Many of the South's volunteers were driven by moral duty and the will to protect their own family and their home; slavery had nothing much to do with most of the desires and aspirations in taking up the cause of this struggle. Even the North, initially, was fighting the South not to put paid to slavery as such but to prevent the Southern states from seceding, as this was thought to be a direct attack on the Constitution. The argument of slavery or abolition was in fact quite by the way even though, with its characteristic way of taking short cuts, the collective memory of both Europe and the United States is quite convinced today, that it was indeed a weighty argument at the time.

The struggle against slavery, unlike what legend and historical shortcuts have led us to believe nowadays, was far from being a major quarrel and wasn't even one of the reasons for the conflict itself. On 4 July 1861, Abraham Lincoln (1809-65), elected in 1860, in a message addressed to Congress, stated that he had *"no purpose, directly or indirectly, to interfere with slavery in the States where it exists."* [1] With the exception of the radicals who wanted a war against slavery, the Union wanted to wage war mainly because the idea of Secession was anticonstitutional. Congress resolutions dated 22 and 25 July confirmed and underlined that the object of the steps taken to wage war was not of "overthrowing or interfering the rights and the established institutions by the [seceded] States" but rather *"to defend and maintain the supremacy of the Constitution and to preserve the Union with all the dignity, the equality and the rights of the various States unimpaired."* [2]

But in spite of the strength of their convictions it has to be remembered that at the beginning of the conflict, neither side was really ready to go to war. Improvisation, more or less cloaked in romantic and idealist visions of war, and the absence of any real foresight and planning were the key words which described the two belligerents,

For all that, the war was just as fratricidal. President Jefferson (1808-1889) for the Southern states and Abraham Lincoln, the President of the Union, both came from Kentucky. This was in itself a perfect example of the real division among the American people, because the inhabitants of Kentucky took literally opposite positions in more or less equal proportions (more than 2/5 of the white men fought in the Confederate ranks). On the other hand in Missouri, 3/4 of the whites, like 2/3 of the whites in Maryland, joined the Union ranks.

During the fever of the first months following the call to arms the rush of volunteers was considerable, to such an extent that it revealed even more how poorly organised the logistics of the armies being

Below.
The Confederate cabinet united around President Davis, sitting in the centre, at the moment war was declared.
(RR)

P TO THE BATTLE

1. In James M. McPherson: Battle Cry for Freedom – the American Civil War, *Oxford University Press, Inc. 1988, page 312 (Penguin Edition).*
Translator's note: for simplicity's sake the Penguin Edition of this book has been used for the quotations. Pascal Le Pautremat originally used the French translation published as La Guerre de Séccession, Editions Robert Laffont, Collection Bouquins, 1991

2. James M. McPherson, op. cit., p 312 (Penguin Edition) from a logistical, material, as well as a strategic and tactical point of view. All the more so as at the beginning of 1861 almost one third of the officers in the National army resigned to join the Southern forces; this was not counting those who, exasperated by the bureaucratic routines of the army before and at the outset of the war, had hunga up their uniforms once and for all, in order to prosper in civilian life; so that in fact the Ministry of War had no strategic plan nor any mobilisation programme at the beginning of the conflict. Things were only set up gradually.

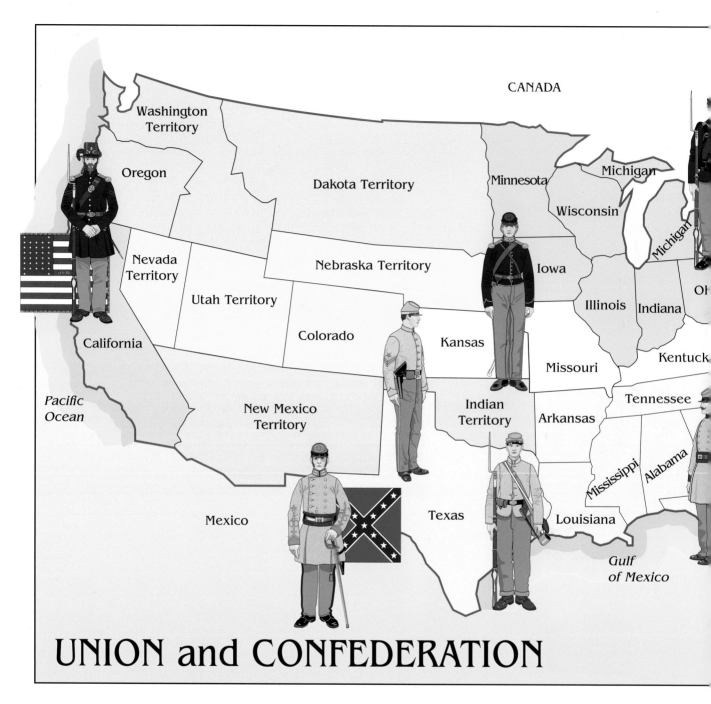

UNION and CONFEDERATION

built up were. Once hostilities had broken out, the Union States were able to muster some 2.1 million soldiers and sailors.

As far as the number of volunteers recruited by the South is concerned, this can only be estimated since the Southern states' archives were almost all destroyed at the end of the conflict. According to the sources it is thought that the Confederate states were able to field between 600 000 and 1.4 million men.

But it is more commonly thought that 850 000 to 900 000 men wore the grey uniform.

THE FORCES PRESENT IN THE MIDST OF THE POLITICAL AND ECONOMIC STAKES

In the spring of 1861 the large numbers of soldiers which were typical of the coming years were a long way from all being assembled. The Seceding states from the High South supplied a total of

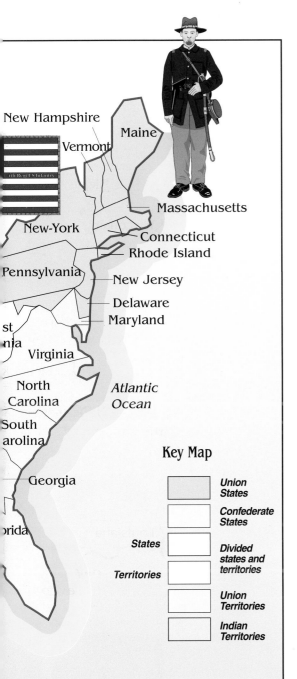

New Hampshire

Maine

Vermont

Massachusetts

New-York

Connecticut

Rhode Island

Pennsylvania

New Jersey

Delaware

Maryland

st
nia

Virginia

North
Carolina

*Atlantic
Ocean*

South
arolina

Georgia

rida

Key Map

States		***Union States***
		Confederate States
		Divided states and territories
Territories		***Union Territories***
		Indian Territories

mobilise the troops, it has to be said that the solid structures which any army needs were far from set up in the North: no general staff headquarters, no strategic plan, no serious military map making. The Union cartographers, who had no maps of the South, were saved by General Henry Wager Halleck (1815-1872), at first responsible for the Western Front, then Commanding General of the Union forces between 1862 and 1864; he very quickly went and bought some maps in a Saint-Louis bookshop, which in itself was a valuable initiative for the sizeable plan which was being set in motion for the South by Washington.

Apart from their practical shortcomings, the military themselves also showed how strikingly lacking in combat experience they were.

Most of the Union officers had never commanded in battle; most of them came from commerce or from business except for two seventy-year-olds, veterans of the Mexican War (1846-1848), among whom General Winfield Scott Hancock (1824-1886), himself a Virginian in the service of the Union. On the Navy side, out of the 42 Union warships, only a dozen were directly available to operate along the East coast, even though Lincoln had ordered Confederate ports to be blockaded on 19 April 1861. [3]

Moreover, officers defecting from the Union army and joining the Confederate troops only highlighted the unease and the pernicious frame of mind among Yankee troops; their strength was established at only about 150 000 recruits in April 1861. Out of the 1 098 officers listed in April 1961, 371 went over to the Southern camp including General Robert Lee (1807-1870), a graduate of West Point and second of his year in 1829, whose job it was to command the North Virginia Army before becoming Commander-in-Chief of the Confederate troops.

Below.
This heavy fortress canon – probably a XXX-lb canon – mounted on a fixed carriage – note that the wheels can still be used belonging to the battery defending a fortress, at the beginning of the conflict. The gunners belong to the Union.
(RR)

425 000 men according to the estimates, or half the total Confederate strength. As proof of the deep rift in people's convictions, these same states supplied 235 000 whites and 85 000 blacks to the Union's forces, bearing in mind that generally the blacks only represented 15% of all Union troops.

IMPROVISING AND UNPREPARED

Apart from the goodwill and the effort made to

THE UNION INFANTRY

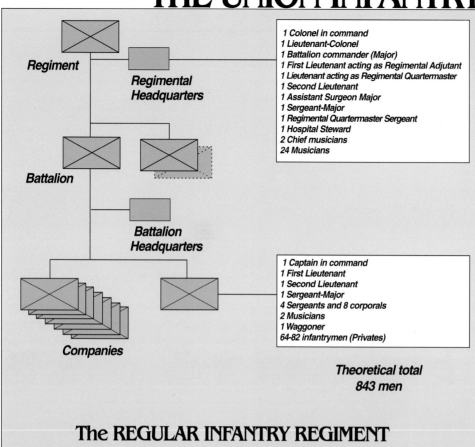

Regiment

Regimental
Headquarters

1 Colonel in command
1 Lieutenant-Colonel
1 Battalion commander (Major)
1 First Lieutenant acting as Regimental Adjutant
1 Lieutenant acting as Regimental Quartermaster
1 Second Lieutenant
1 Assistant Surgeon Major
1 Sergeant-Major
1 Regimental Quartermaster Sergeant
1 Hospital Steward
2 Chief musicians
24 Musicians

Battalion

Battalion
Headquarters

1 Captain in command
1 First Lieutenant
1 Second Lieutenant
1 Sergeant-Major
4 Sergeants and 8 corporals
2 Musicians
1 Waggoner
64-82 infantrymen (Privates)

Companies

Theoretical total
843 men

The REGULAR INFANTRY REGIMENT

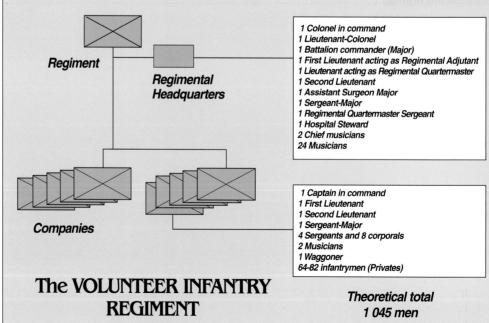

Regiment

Regimental
Headquarters

1 Colonel in command
1 Lieutenant-Colonel
1 Battalion commander (Major)
1 First Lieutenant acting as Regimental Adjutant
1 Lieutenant acting as Regimental Quartermaster
1 Second Lieutenant
1 Assistant Surgeon Major
1 Sergeant-Major
1 Regimental Quartermaster Sergeant
1 Hospital Steward
2 Chief musicians
24 Musicians

Companies

1 Captain in command
1 First Lieutenant
1 Second Lieutenant
1 Sergeant-Major
4 Sergeants and 8 corporals
2 Musicians
1 Waggoner
64-82 infantrymen (Privates)

The VOLUNTEER INFANTRY
REGIMENT

Theoretical total
1 045 men

THE WAR STARTS
FT. SUMTER, S. C.—APR. 12, 1861

UNION TROOPS AND THEIR POTENTIAL

To increase the number of regular troops, President Abraham Lincoln quickly called for a levy of 175 000 volunteers, the first in a series of similar decisions. As the lack of numbers remained a constant problem during the following months, conscription was finally adopted in July 1963 for the 18-35 age group in the Union population that numbered almost 19 million people. There were a lot of exemptions however, so much so that in the end, only 6% of this age group actually served under the flag, the others managing to get themselves replaced for money.

In the volunteer regiments [4], the men elected their captains and lieutenants. Other officers, at their own expense, formed units from nothing and the men they had themselves recruited then not surprisingly elected them.

The Navy corps was weakened by 373 navy officers out of the 1 554 listed defecting to the Southern camp. That being said, the North had the advantage of concentrating most of the naval shipyards, against the South's only one. This turned out to be a determining factor for the duration of the war. Finally the Navy succeeded in offsetting its lack of warships by purchasing merchant ships that it armed and put into service with the blockade. At the end of 1861, the Union thus had more than 260 warships, with another hundred or so being built.

In Washington, although all the administration was also caught with its pants down, just like the South, the advantage obtained from the Northern states' industrial potential greatly played in favour of setting the war effort in motion in the shortest possible time. But unlike the South, the military and civilian authorities were far from being effective and competent, just like the Minister for War, Simon Cameron (1799-1889) who, according to numerous sources, was terribly incompetent just like a large part of the civil service everybody thought was almost fossilised.

And above all, the North delayed mobilising enough of its troops even though, it is estimated, it had more than three and a half times more white men of service age than the South.

*Above.
It was at Fort Sumter on 12 April 1861 that, hostilities were started between the North and the South. On the 13th, the Union garrison lay down its arms after more than thirty hours of Confederate artillery bombardment.
(RR)*

4. In theory a regiment, Union or Confederate, had a strength of a thousand soldiers in ten companies. A brigade numbered four regiments, or 4 000 men on average; and there were three or four brigades per division, or 12 000 men; two divisions or three to make up an army corps, or 24 000 men minimum. In reality, the organigram of the Union forces never reached such numbers because of the different levels of training.

75 000 militiamen were nonetheless mobilised for ninety days' service, applying an old 1795 law. Then on 3 May, Lincoln called for a further 42 000 volunteers to be mobilised together with 18 000 sailors for a period of three years. This decision, taken by the President without consulting Congress as was his right as Supreme Commander of the Army and Navy, was ratified by Congress in July which, in addition, called for a million volunteers to be mobilised for three years. So much so that at the beginning of 1862, the Union army could count on more than 700 000 soldiers, of whom 90 000 were enrolled for a period of ninety days and who for the most part withdrew for three years.

In fact, although the volunteers were far from being negligible in the North, the capacity for managing and supplying clothing, weapons, ammunition, and wagons for them was greatly below what was needed and expected. At this stage it was the States which, with the local authorities and the citizens' goodwill worked all throughout 1861 to make up for the delay and the deficiencies in their logistics, going so far as to equip certain regiments from head to foot themselves. The result was, just like in the South, a host of uniforms and colours which made for a rather motley gathering, or even something close to a circus parade, during official assemblies. Medical examinations at the time of recruitment were however less stringent so that

with hindsight it is thought that in 1861 some 25% of the volunteers should have been declared unfit for service.

Everything sorted itself out from 1862 onwards, though the Union did have to ensure the security of its supply routes as it progressed through Southern territory by protecting the railways, roads and port installations. The Battle of Bull Run also illustrates in condensed form the restrictions and imperatives which could be imposed upon an army, bearing in mind that on average an army of 100 000 men needed 2 500 logistics wagons and 35 000 animals, with average daily food consumption fixed at 600 tonnes.

THE CONFEDERATES: THE OBVIOUS DISADVANTAGES

The problem of numbers was almost the same as for the Union, except that the Confederacy adopted conscription earlier, in April 1862, one year after the beginning of the conflict. Although at the beginning, the 18-35 age group was also concerned, conscription was finally extended to men of fifty in 1864, given the serious situation the Confederate cause found itself in.

Jefferson Davis logically called up the militiamen, or rather more exactly the companies of volunteers who, ever since 1850, had replaced them. This did not lessen the need for volunteers in the first weeks of the war.

On 6 March 1861, the Confederate Congress authorised the formation of an army of 100 000 volunteers for twelve months' service. These volunteer regiments were in fact equipped and armed

THE CONFEDERATE INFANTRY

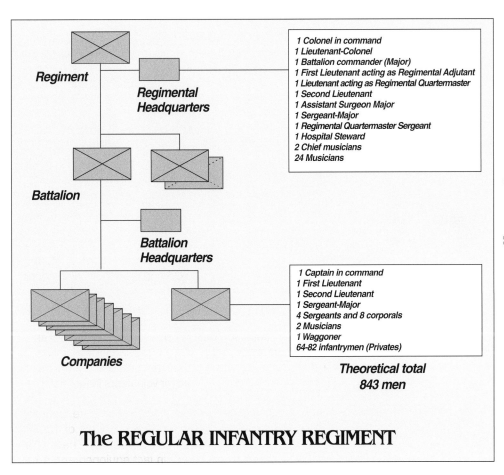

Regiment

Regimental Headquarters

1 Colonel in command
1 Lieutenant-Colonel
1 Battalion commander (Major)
1 First Lieutenant acting as Regimental Adjutant
1 Lieutenant acting as Regimental Quartermaster
1 Second Lieutenant
1 Assistant Surgeon Major
1 Sergeant-Major
1 Regimental Quartermaster Sergeant
1 Hospital Steward
2 Chief musicians
24 Musicians

Battalion

Battalion Headquarters

1 Captain in command
1 First Lieutenant
1 Second Lieutenant
1 Sergeant-Major
4 Sergeants and 8 corporals
2 Musicians
1 Waggoner
64-82 infantrymen (Privates)

Companies

**Theoretical total
843 men**

The REGULAR INFANTRY REGIMENT

by the States, or the municipalities or even rich donators, because the Richmond authorities were incapable of fulfilling this nonetheless essential task. After Fort Sumter fell on 12 April 1861 – the event which strictly speaking marked the beginning of open hostilities in the Civil War – a further 60 000 men were enrolled.

Then in spite of the difficulties and shortfalls in equipment and supplies, in May 1861, Congress ordered 400 000 other volunteers to be mobilised for a period of three years. Because of a lack of equipment, only about 200 000 volunteers were accepted and enrolled under the flag.

The rest were sent back home because they could not be properly equipped. Weapons anyway were all assorted, with rifled gun barrels being rare at the beginning of the conflict and especially at the Battle of Manassas. The problem was also compounded by the fact that the elected Confederate representatives clamoured for forces to be held at

several border points for fear of the Union hordes overwhelming them; this meant that the Southern forces were to a certain degree dispersed, spread out along a long, defensive cordon without any proper depth.

The advantage for the South was that it disposed of men who were more used to the country and therefore campaign life than the Unionists: they were more rural because of their professional activities which were inherent to the farming world and its various activities.

Apart from its land capabilities, the Confederacy had also to look after its naval means and build up a hitherto non-existent fleet. Like with the army, the Confederacy took advantage of good quality sailors rallying its cause. All the authorities had to do was to arm the merchant vessels, convert tugs and launches into gun-boats, and get semi-submersible torpedo boats operational.

They were relying on using mines to protect the

ports. Finally, the Confederacy also had recourse to corsairs, with a degree of success.

When the South mobilised, the militia regiments reinforced the Confederate troops. Grey was chosen as the official colour even though this hue had until then been retained for officer cadets only. Despite this, and especially at Bull Run, the Confederate troops displayed rather a variety of uniforms and colours. Even the weapons were a long way from being standardised. The Southern states in addition suffered from a dearth of foundries; there was only one, the Tredegar foundry for the heavy materiel (cannon).

As for producing rifles, they could only rely on the little Richmond and Fayettesville foundries, in

North Carolina. The powder was made at Pont in Delaware. As a result the Southerners had to import most of the powder and saltpetre they needed and try to get it through the blockade.

In fact in both camps, the initial logistics was very far from being satisfactory, its shortcomings even going so far as food shortages for the soldiers, above all the Southerners who were fairly frequently subjected to this problem because they didn't have effective or sufficient means of transport even though the storehouses were well supplied. To sum up, the Confederate Materiel Department was deplorable, despite the efforts of Josiah Gorgas (1818-1883) who took over in April 1861. Gorgas showed great energy by despatching intermediaries to Euro-

Above, from left to right. These two shots show officers from the 14th Louisiana Infantry Regiment at the beginning of the war. It is sometimes difficult to distinguish between the civilian frock coats and the regulation tunics worn by officers on both sides, be they regulars or volunteers. (RR)

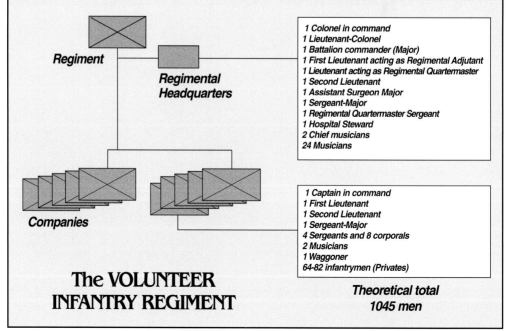

Regiment

Regimental Headquarters

1 Colonel in command
1 Lieutenant-Colonel
1 Battalion commander (Major)
1 First Lieutenant acting as Regimental Adjutant
1 Lieutenant acting as Regimental Quartermaster
1 Second Lieutenant
1 Assistant Surgeon Major
1 Sergeant-Major
1 Regimental Quartermaster Sergeant
1 Hospital Steward
2 Chief musicians
24 Musicians

Companies

1 Captain in command
1 First Lieutenant
1 Second Lieutenant
1 Sergeant-Major
4 Sergeants and 8 corporals
2 Musicians
1 Waggoner
64-82 infantrymen (Privates)

The VOLUNTEER INFANTRY REGIMENT

Theoretical total 1045 men

Confederate Generals and headquarters staff

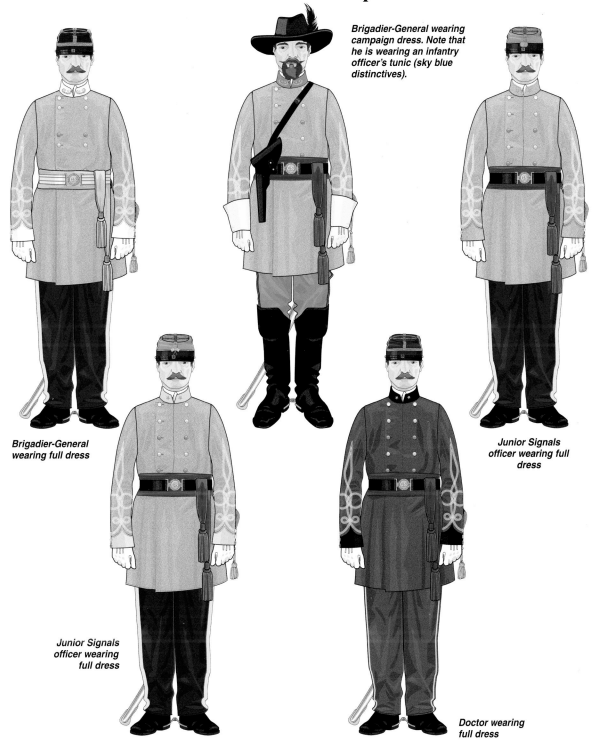

Brigadier-General wearing campaign dress. Note that he is wearing an infantry officer's tunic (sky blue distinctives).

Brigadier-General wearing full dress

Junior Signals officer wearing full dress

Junior Signals officer wearing full dress

Doctor wearing full dress

pe, among whom Caleb Huse (1831-1905), to buy arms and ammunition, whilst James Dunwoody Bulloch (1823-1901), an intelligence expert and head of a lobby in England, tried to get warships built in Queen Victoria's shipyards. 1861 and the beginning of 1862 were greatly influenced by these valuable importations for the Southerners.

Gorgas got down to developing heavy industry capacity in the Southern states, with notably the creation of arsenals and foundries for producing arms and cannon. A large powder factory was set up at Augusta and started production in 1862. Officers from the Materiel Department went back and forth across the Southern states recovering copper for building the primers, multiplying their efforts to get church and plantation bells melted down for making cannon.

They even went so far as to recover used lead from the battlefields to recycle it, together with discarded and damaged weapons; these efforts were to pay off and were decisive in 1863 and especially in 1864.

But for the time being, at the time of Bull Run-Manassas, even though the efforts in all departments had been set in motion, they still had to produce results and the immediate context was that

the troops remained rather destitute, equipped with different models of weapons of varying quality.

In the South, because of Governors who were anxious to protect their own territories, the scarcity of weapons if not the repeated obstacles to redistributing the stocks from the Confederate arsenals was such that the soldiers held their Minister of War, Leroy Pope Walker (1817-1884), who was considered imbecile and negligent, for responsible. He ended up resigning shortly after Manassas in September 1861 and was replaced by Judah Philip Benjamin (1811-1884).

These are just as many elements one has to bear in mind when considering the conditions under which both the Union and the Confederate soldiers fought the Battle of Manassas.

Finally it must be emphasised that the feeling commonly shared by both the North and the South was that the war would be short-lived and not very intense. Each side was convinced that they would very quickly win. In the North, the military and political leaders promoted the idea of a campaign especially intended to suppress the Southerners' effrontery and put an end to the rebellion. In the South it was a question of struggling with conviction and resolve to safeguard their society.

After all is said and done, as the American historian, James M. McPherson underlines *"The South could "win" the war by not losing; the North could only win by winning. The large territory of the confederacy – 750 000 square miles, as large as Russia west of Moscow, twice the size of the thirteen original United States – would make Lincoln's task as difficult as Napoleon's in 1812 or George III's in 1776."* [5]

The battle of Manassas made everybody adopt a more realistic and pragmatic approach to war, which admittedly does consist of din and ferocity, but also of dead and wounded, of rout or victory; this approach was acquired in the course of either unforeseen events or following a succession of factors which, all put together, tipped the balance in favour of one or the other sides.

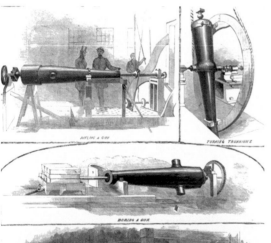

5. James M. McPherson: Battle Cry for Freedom – the American Civil War, Oxford University Press, Inc. 1988, page 337 (Penguin Edition)

Confederate Volunteers

**11th Mississippi
Volunteers Infantry**

**1st Louisiana
Battalion**

**5th Louisiana
Volunteers Infantry**

**Junior Officer from the
11th Virginia Volunteers
Infantry**

**17th Virginia Volunteers
Infantry, Alexandria Rifles**

Confederate Regular Infantry

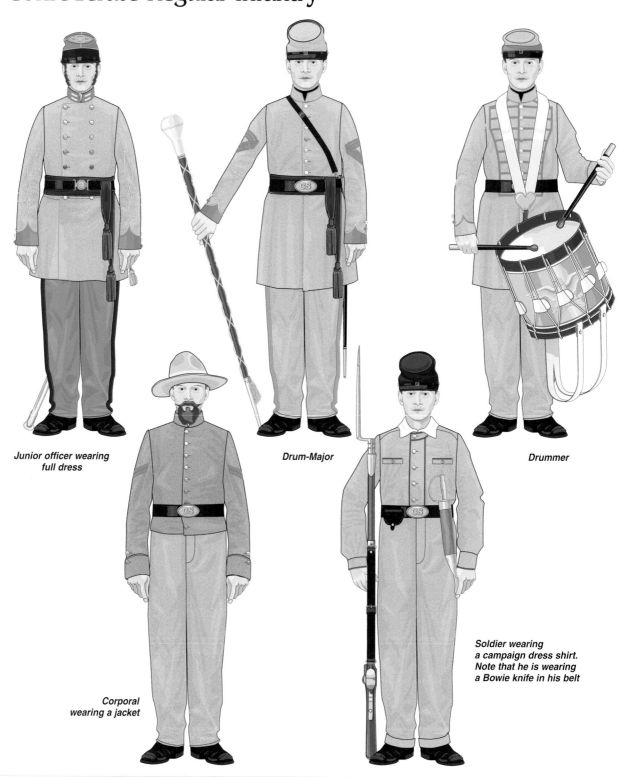

Junior officer wearing
full dress

Drum-Major

Drummer

Corporal
wearing a jacket

Soldier wearing
a campaign dress shirt.
Note that he is wearing
a Bowie knife in his belt

Confederate Regular Infantry

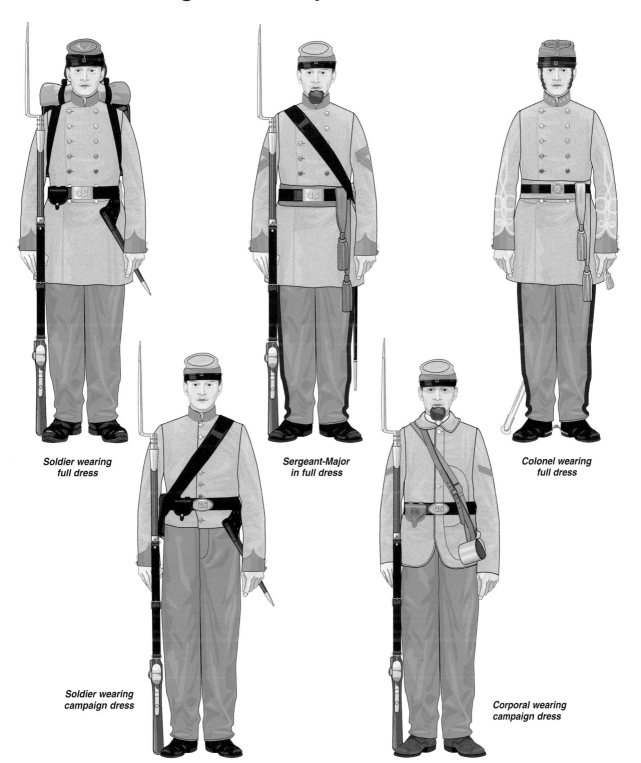

*Soldier wearing
full dress*

*Sergeant-Major
in full dress*

*Colonel wearing
full dress*

*Soldier wearing
campaign dress*

*Corporal wearing
campaign dress*

Confederate Artillery

Gunner wearing campaign dress

Officer and gunner from the Washington Light Artillery

Corporal wearing campaign dress

Armstrong 3-in breech-loading canon imported from Britain

Gunner from the Lynchburg Artillery

Confederate Cavalry

Sergeant-Major
wearing full dress

Corporal wearing
full dress

Trumpeter wearing
full dress

Junior officer
wearing full dress

Trooper from
the 1st Virginia Cavalry

T HE BATTLE OF MANASSAS WAS THE FIRST MAJOR CONFRONTATION between the two sides, and what was more in a state, Virginia, which became like a go-between area between the North and the South, a highly strategic crossroad region of which both sides were well aware.

THE IMPORTANCE OF VIRGINIA

Right.
The President of the Confederate States of America, the former Democrat Senator for Mississippi, Jefferson Davis, elected to this post on 18 February 1861.
(RR)

Below, from left to right.
The Township of Centreville, a railway junction and the object of everyone's desire. The panorama on the left shows the town before the battle. Note on the right the fort defending the main access to the town.

On the right hand picture, the artist has shown the approaches to the railway on the way into to Centreville a few days after the battle.
(RR)

The Confederacy knew perfectly well that it could not outdo the North's numerical and industrial advantage forever. At the same time, a war of attrition waged against Washington was not in tune with the psychology of the South's fighting men; what they wanted was to launch themselves into an attack against the enemy. The Confederate strategists therefore decided to make use as much as possible of defensive operations and to use intensively the lines of communication already available in their zone of influence.

Indeed from the strategic and political standpoint, the Confederacy relied principally on a solid policy of defending and consolidating its territorial base, by preparing to drive off any Union offensives, but without itself thinking of launching a campaign to invade the North. The leaders hoped to reverse the situation with foreign intervention and by weakening the Unionists at their own game by blocking their offensives.

The Federation of Northern States in fact had no other choice but to launch a series of offensives aimed at breaking Southern resistance and effrontery. But to do that, before anything else, it had to build up a sizeable army by getting round the type of military service lasting only three months which had been set up for a good number of young men of the period. A truly permanent army had to be formed and led with intelligence and strategy. This strategy

also included the perspective of blockading the southern ports in order to stifle the South economically. The need to operate quickly and decisively made General Hancock hit out as circumstances dictated against the Mississippi and more especially Virginia, given the proximity of the two opposing capitals, Washington and Richmond, only about eighty miles apart, and over territory crossed by rivers with such evocative names like James, York, Rappahannock, Potomac, Chickahominy, North and South Anna and the Bull Run. Everything seemed to make Virginia the region where a lot of operations would be carried out. The terrain was flat and wooded, relieved by hills and mountains, with the great Shenandoah Valley running north-east to south-west.

This valley was considered strategic by the Southerners in so far as it opened out into Maryland and Pennsylvania, beyond the Potomac. It constituted an axis that could be used to break through, enabling them to cut the lines of communications with Washington. On the other hand for the Unionists, the valley was of little importance. In fact, for the Confederates, attacking Washington turned

out to be easy, both from the south and from the west, unlike the Unionists operating against Richmond. The Unionists only had one choice in fact: either directly via Fredericksburg, or by the sea route from the peninsula.

These were therefore the strategic reasons for the Union penetrating Virginia. Indeed the Baltimore-Ohio railway line became of capital importance since it passed through the state, just like the River Ohio, along its border for almost 190 miles. This railway line was the most direct logistics link between the capital of the Union, Washington, and the Mid-West states. This had not escaped the Confederates who, from a purely logically guerrilla point of view, had got down to cutting the line in several places, notably at Harper's Ferry, as well as at Grafton in West Virginia, an important railway junction situated sixty or so miles to the south of Wheeling. Hence the Virginians' appeals to Washington for help. Because they did not obtain enough troops from the capital, worried as it was for its own safety, it was the governor of Ohio, William Dennison (1815-82) who brought in military aid, relying especially on the soldiers

Left.
General Robert E. Lee. At first opposed to the idea of the Southern States seceding, he joined the armed forces of Virginia of which he was a loyal citizen. He was appointed General in Chief of the troops of the State of Virginia a few weeks after he resigned from the Union Army in April 1861. He was one of the first five generals of the Confederate States of the South before becoming their General in Chief a few months before the surrender in 1865.
(RR)

and the competence of George B. McClellan (1826-85), who was back in uniform as Commandant of the Ohio Militia; William S. Rosencrans (1819-98), his former aide de camp, appointed Brigadier-General in May 1861, both of them graduating from West Point among the best in their year; and Jacob Dolson Cox (1828-1900), at the time Brigadier-General. All three of them had the particularity of having been in business before donning their uniforms again with the imminence of civil war. McClellan, then aged 30, had left the army in 1857 to return in 1861. And in the spring of 1961, they were all at the head of regiments they had carefully organised themselves.

May started with both sides endeavouring to reinforce their defence potential. At the beginning of June, President Jefferson Davis could rely on the 22 000 men under General Pierre G.T. de Beauregard (1818-93), the victor of Fort Sumter, very Napoleonic in his attitud and his way of thinking; his men were in fact positioned at Manassas Junction, a major railroad junction less than 30 miles southwest of Washington, together with the 11 000 men under Joseph E. Johnston, a small and always impeccably dressed man, located at Winchester. Facing these two forces who could join up in a couple of hours, were the 35 000 men that the Union general, Winfield Scott Hancock, had entrusted to his former staff officer, Irvin McDowell (1818-85), who had no direct experience of command in the field. Made a Brigadier-General in May 1861, McDowell was thus at the head of the North-Eastern Virginia regular army with Arlington as its headquarters. He set himself up around Centerville in Virginia. To his own forces he could attach General Paterson's at Harper's Ferry. Their forces were therefore separated by a few days' march. But the relative nearness of both Confederate forces to each other, together with the support of the railway, played a decisive role on the course of this first Battle of Bull Run.

Confederate flags

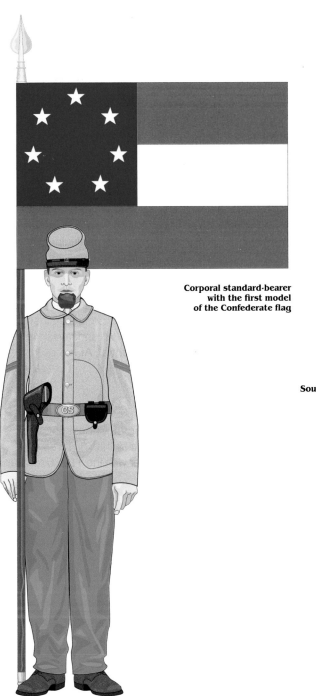

**Corporal standard-bearer
with the first model
of the Confederate flag**

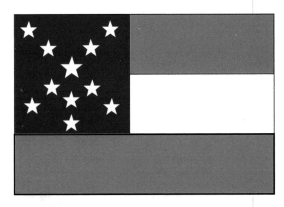

**Mississippi
regimental flag**

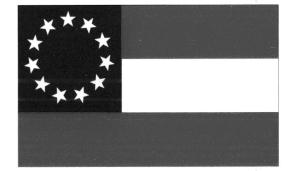

Southern States flag

**Virginia
regimental flag**

Opposite.
**President Abraham
Lincoln, a fervent
republican, the sym-
bol of the struggle
against slavery and
the durability of the
state.**

Right.
**General Scott
Hancock, the author
of the plan which
the Union General
Staff applied: limited
action combined
with a blockade.**
(RR)

THE UNION'S OPERATIONAL PLANS

A short time before Bull Run General Scott Hancock, bearing in mind the destruction that war causes, was known to oppose an invasion. On the contrary he was in favour of limited action and especially of a systematic blockade as a way of neutralising the Southerners' rather vague aspirations and thus avoid the humiliation and vexations provoked by a war of conquest which would also be murderous and destructive; a conquest that would, according to him, risk rousing Southerners' bitterness for generations to come.

GENERAL SCOTT'S PROJECT: COMBINING LIMITED ACTION WITH A BLOCKADE

With his plan, General Scott wanted at all cost to avoid haste. In his preparations he was in close contact with General McClellan. In his correspondence with Hancock, particularly that of 27 April 1861, McClellan suggested launching a vast offensive with almost 80 000 men from Ohio and the north of Mississippi and carrying out a truly large-scale attack eastwards following the Great Kanawha Valley towards Virginia, heading for Richmond. Failing that, he recommended going down through Tennessee towards the town of Montgomery. He also recommended combined action eastwards to Charleston and to Georgia, the aim being to reach the coast of the Gulf of Mexico and in particular the towns of Mobile (Alabama), Pensacola, New

Orleans and Florida. According to him Richmond had to be reached as quickly as possible. In fact Hancock in a reply dated 3 May, stated that he preferred to take the seceding states one after the other, but also that he wanted to keep to a precise plan: i.e. blockading the coast, using naval means on the Mississippi but also, by means of an amphibious operation, getting hold of New Orleans. The idea also was to hold the Mississippi, which he considered to be a truly vital means of communication.

In order to carry out his plan successfully, he recommended that the volunteers receive several months' training and that river gunboats be built so that he could to launch his operation in mid-November 1861.

Although his operation was kept strictly secret, the Northern press finally managed to get wind of the basic plan. The press derided his plan for its limited action and a blockade, and called it the Anaconda plan because of the twisted nature of its tactics. Although quite ignorant of the art of war the Northern population demanded quick and effective results, and clamoured for a repressive invasion to be carried out speedily. This was the reason therefore why the Yankee effort made at the beginning of July took the form of a large-scale operation against Southern troops, protecting the railway junction at Manassas in the north of Virgi-

Right.
***Putting the plans in operation
and the Union armies' aborted attempts.***

nia, linking the Shenandoah Valley with the rest of Southern territory.

After Hancock's plan had been given a thinly disguised disavowal by the Union side, George B. McClellan at 34, full of himself and aware of his capacities and his qualities as a strategist and a tactician, thought he could obtain support for his own plan. McClellan had already illustrated himself in the Mexican War, as an officer of Engineers at the age of only 20. At the same time, according to his contemporaries, he tended to have a pessimistic view of the events he went through, always overestimated his adversary and hesitated to use all his forces. Besides on 26 May 1861, McClellan launched his men against a 1 500 strong Confederate detachment holding Grafton. The Colonel of the Rebel unit preferred to withdraw his men towards Philippeville, some fifteen miles further south.

They were however pursued by some 3 000 Union soldiers launched upon a forced march in the rain by night and along barely practicable roads.

Meanwhile General Lee was at Richmond, retained there by his responsibilities as Commander-in-Chief of the Virginia armed forces. It was impossible for him to send massive reinforcements to confront George B. McClellan's troops, apart from

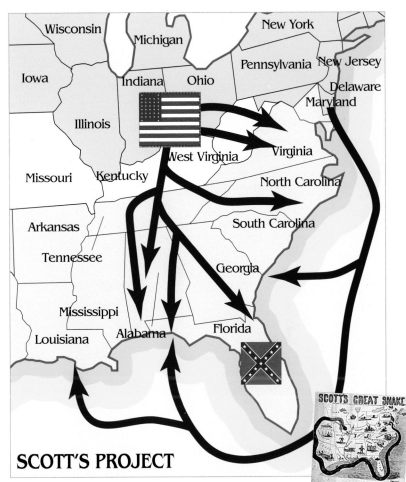

SCOTT'S PROJECT

Opposite, from left to right.
General McClellan: too pessimistic and too unsure of himself, he became general in chief and inhibited the Union armies for many long months.
(RR)

General Irvin McDowell (1818-85) succeeded in imposing his strategic views on President Lincoln, which were in favour of invading Virginia. But his plan, which was launched too late, ran into the Battle of Bull Run and a bitter failure.
(RR)

29

times, praising their merit and their bravery with a certain pomposity.

But alongside McClellan's agitations, for several weeks now Washington had been analysing and weighing up the plan put forward by General McDowell to the Department of War. His project consisted of total and immediate action against the enemy to take control of the whole of Virginia. In his manoeuvre he planned to attack the 20 000 Confederate soldiers who were defending Manassas junction on the flank, while relying on the 15 000 Union troops under Robert Patterson, gathered at Harper's Ferry, to prevent the 11 000 Confederates facing them from reinforcing their comrades at Manassas. In fact he wanted to defeat General Beauregard who had positioned his army less than 35 miles from Washington, near Manassas. According to intelligence, he estimated Beauregard's forces at 25 000 men, knowing that General John Eggleston Johnston (1807-91) also commanded 30 000 to 35 000 men in the Shenandoah Valley. McDowell was aware of the fact that Beauregard could be reinforced thanks to the railway line from the Valley to Manassas.

According to the plan put forward by McDowell, it was a question of blocking Johnston using the troops situated north of the Potomac while he mar-

These sketches made at the beginning of the conflict by a New York artist show the variety of uniforms worn by the Northern army volunteers. Despite what Hollywood depicts in its films, the uniforms are very similar to those worn in Europe or in Latin America at the same time.

Top, left: an officer from the 7th New York Volunteer Regiment. Right: a volunteer from New York wearing a very Crimean War-style greatcoat. Bottom: a horse gunner from the Light Artillery wearing full dress. (Private Collection, RR)

4 500 men under Adjutant-General Robert Selden Garnett, soldiers with very varied uniforms and disorderly because they were not disciplined. Garnett nonetheless succeeded in closing off the passes through which passed the roads running from the Shenandoah Valley to the towns of Wheeling and Parkersburg.

MCDOWELL'S AMBITION AND A RESOLUTELY OFFENSIVE PLAN

At the end of June 1861, General McClellan could now count on a reinforced strength of some 25 000 men of whom almost 6 000 were concentrated on the protection of the *B & O railway* line which had been reopened up in the direction of Washington. The Union advances caused a measured withdrawal by the Southern forces in Virginia; this was considered in Washington as a notable success, a success that McClellan did not hesitate to make the most of by putting himself forward and identifying himself – consciously or not – with Napoleon. In that capacity he heckled his soldiers several

Union General Staff and Generals

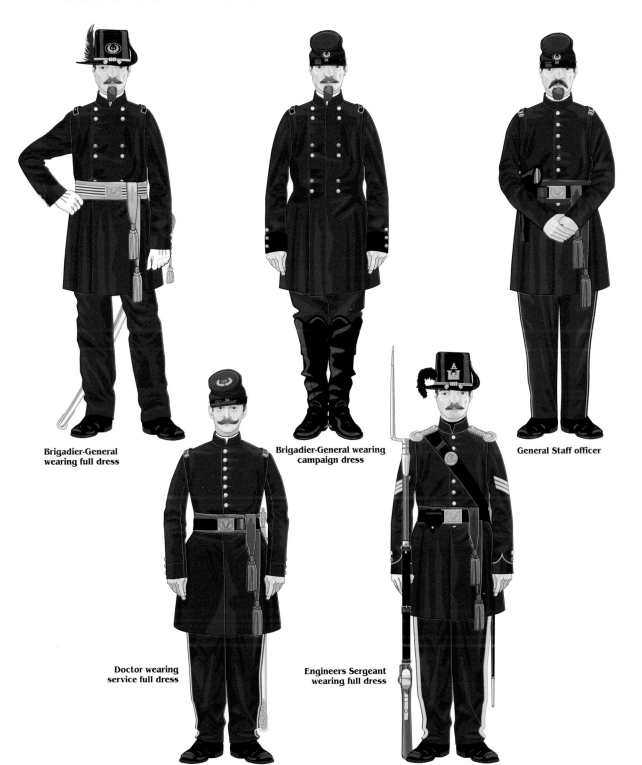

Brigadier-General wearing full dress

Brigadier-General wearing campaign dress

General Staff officer

Doctor wearing service full dress

Engineers Sergeant wearing full dress

Union Infantry: Regular Army

Soldier wearing full dress

Drummer

Junior officer wearing full dress

Fife-player. The regimental band was made up of other musicians wearing the same uniform.

Drum-Major. Note that he is wearing two re-engagement stripes, i.e. ten years' service.

Union Infantry: Volunteers

69th New York Volunteers
Infantry

Colonel of the 1st Rhode
Island Infantry

79th New York Volunteers
infantry.

39th New York Volunteers
infantry.

Sergeant of the 3rd Maine
Volunteers infantry.

Union Infantry: Regular Army

Soldier wearing campaign
dress

Corporal wearing
campaign dress

Soldier wearing campaign
dress

Junior officers wearing
campaign dress

ched against Beauregard with a column of 30 000 men and a reserve of some 10 000 others. Knowing moreover that his militia regiments were untrained and their officers inexperienced, McDowell suggested splitting the troops up into little brigades, each led by a colonel and junior officers from the regular army.

On 29 June, Lincoln showed some interest in McDowell's plan, so much so that he assembled his cabinet and his military advisers at the White House. As a matter of course General Hancock, no doubt concentrating on his own plan, turned McDowell's plan down considering it impractical. Even though Scott Hancock was motivated partly by jealousy, his criticism was no less warranted since such a plan, although quite feasible for professional troops, was too risky for a force of amateurs.

But the President and his cabinet were afire with impatience to get to the heart of the matter. A number of Union politicians thought that it was a race against time when they learnt that the Confederate government had set up the city of Richmond as its capital in and that a new session of the Southern Congress was due to start on 20 July 1861. Hence the number of calls for action published in the press, like in Horace Greeley's New York Tribune which called for Richmond to be taken in the shortest delay. They also wanted to transpose the successful tactics inherent in the Mexican War to Virginia – namely a brutal invasion until the capital was captured. Lincoln finally rallied to the prevailing atmosphere of optimism and considered it was opportune to attack the Rebels at Manassas, thinking that this would be a limited, small-scale operation and that it could be carried out conjointly with the blockade process which was being put into place gradually and which became effective

Above.
These three studio photographs show the reality of the uniforms, the attitudes and the faces of the protagonists in the Civil War very well. Union infantryman, Southern trooper or a volunteer from one of the Northern states, there was not very much to differentiate them.
(Private Collection, RR)

Below.
At the beginning of the conflict on both sides, as this little frieze shows, Light Infantrymen, Chasseurs "à Pied "and Zouaves "à la française" were the fashion. It was sometimes difficult to recognise which side was which.
(RR)

Union Artillery: Regular Army

Corporal wearing full
dress 3rd US Artillery.

Corporal wearing
campaign dress

Trooper in the Light
Artillery wearing a jacket

Junior officer
wearing full dress

Junior officer wearing
campaign dress

in 1862. Once Manassas was under control, Lincoln thought that Richmond would become accessible and that this would indeed reduce the duration of the war considerably without destroying Southern territory or increasing human casualties.

Although he was aware that McDowell and his forces lacked experience, Lincoln agreed for the offensive to go ahead. Addressing McDowell he said: "You are a bit of a novice, it's true, but so are they; you're all as much novices as each other." Finally Hancock came round to the position everybody else shared in favour of McDowell's plan which was approved at the very end of June 1861; the launch of the operation was set for 8 July, a delay caused by a lack of wagons and supply problems. They had to act very fast, all the more so, as the High Command knew perfectly well that in mid-July the terms of most of the Ninety-Day militiamen were due to expire, a factor which only stressed the urgent need to gather together substantial reinforcements, equipment and materiel.

The authorities assembled regiments of volunteers, horses, harnesses and wagons, and made up extra trains. At the beginning there were only eight companies of cavalry and almost no Engineers units. It was crucial that McDowell reinforce this capability. McDowell's forces finally started to advance only on 16 July.

The delay was already considerable even before operations started and the consequences were far from being negligible since the Ninety-Day mobilisation period expired on the eve of the Battle of Bull Run. This fact had a considerable psychological impact on the Union troops' fighting spirit, which slumped as an infantry regiment and an artillery battery left the dispositions just before the decisive engagement.

Above.
The Confederate artillery setting itself up in Martinsburg, Virginia while the infantry reinforcements take their place in the trains. The American Civil War, the first quite definitely modern war, saw the use of trains balloons and submarines.
(Private Collection, RR)

Despite their weaknesses the Union troops showed off, persuaded they were all-powerful and in no doubt that they would easily get the better of the Rebel forces that they considered, wrongly, inexperienced and disorganised. In fact they didn't take into account that a number of the Southern troops' officers were among the most competent former Union officers.

Before the Battle of Manassas, various clashes, spread out throughout June and the beginning of July prefigured the difficulty which the Union troops would have to face the encounter on 21 July 1861.

PREMONITORY CLASHES

Opposite.
The first clash of the war is to be credited to General Butler, also the campaign's first defeat...
(RR)

On 10 June 1861, a first clash took place at Big Bethel, a few miles from Yorktown, in Virginia. The fight at Big Bethel had Northern troops under Major-General Benjamin Butler (1818-93) coming to grips with a Southern battery installed near the Big Bethel

Union Cavalry

Trooper wearing
a jacket

Trooper wearing
a greatcoat

Trumpeter in full dress

Junior officers wearing
campaign dress

church, ten or so miles from Butler's positions and thirty five or so miles from Yorktown. The various uniform colours soon complicated the situation and mistakes were therefore fairly frequent. Butler's regiments converging on the Confederate battery failed to recognise each other and ended up shooting at one another. As for the attack launched against the Southern battery itself, it failed piteously, with the Northern soldiers coming under sustained fire. The Union troops finally fell back, returning to their initial positions, leaving behind them almost 66 killed and wounded behind them. As for the Confederates, they only lost eight men in the fighting. Proudly encouraged by their victory, they did not miss the opportunity to show their trophies off in Richmond's shop windows.

It is worth remembering that the period was also marked by the Battle of Rich Mountain where, in order to beat General Garnett's forces, George B. McClellan made his main thrust on 1 July against Rich Mountain with three brigades. On 11 July one of these, made up of regiments from Ohio and Indiana, led by his aide de camp General William Rosencrans, notably launched a flank attack rather than risking a frontal attack against the Southern positions. The attack caused 170 dead and 1 300 wounded and prisoners in the Confederate ranks, against only 60 dead on the Union side. McClellan intervened in support and, misinformed about the outcome of the battle, could not exploit the victory, thus enabling a few thousand Southerners to get away. But almost 500 of them were subsequently captured. As for the Southern soldiers who had remained at Laurel Mountain, they dispersed towards the north and east. The Unionists finished however by catching up with the General Garnett's rearguard on 13 July, at Corrick's Ford. Garnett lost his life, apparently the first general to be killed in the conflict.

With his forces continuing to advance, McDowell

if necessary, destroy the opposing forces if he could but without committing himself too much in depth. But there again, the Northern troops – Ninety-Day recruits – showed very little fighting spirit.

Besides, thinking he had superior forces in front of him Patterson, who had the disagreeable habit of always being drunk, chose to block Johnston's troops. Patterson failed in this task so well that on 18 and 19 July Johnston's men were able to reach Piedmont from Winchester and entrain for Manassas where they reinforced the southern positions in a most decisive way, and thus countered more effectively McDowell's army. These trains were skilfully assembled thanks to the efforts of Brigadier-General Thomas J. Jackson (1824-1863), a ferocious Presbyterian. A cautious man, he actually confiscated the *Baltimore & Ohio Railroad* trains, or almost 44 locomotives and 386 freight wagons. Most were damaged or had even been thrown into the river. This did not prevent him from having forty or so locomotives pulled along the road with horses to the town of Strasburg, to add them to the Manassas Gap Railroad and thus reinforce the Confederation's railroad potential.

On his side, McClellan and his troops could, Johnston thought, turn up from the West and Patterson could also at any moment cross the Potomac and attack him. These combined threats, between the west and the north, made his position particularly uncomfortable and worried him, even though Lee had asked him never to abandon Har-

realised that the other Confederate troops were being held at a distance. To counter them, he was relying on the 14 000 men under Major-General Robert Patterson (1792-1881), aged 69 [6], situated in Maryland on the northern bank of the Potomac in the region of Hagerstown. In fact Patterson's job was to keep Johnston's troops away, confront him

6. A businessman and a veteran of the War of 1812 and the Mexican War, Patterson had joined the Militia.

Union Flags

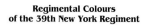

**Regimental Colours
of the 39th New York Regiment**

Regimental Colours of the 1st Pennsylvania Regiment

Regimental Colours of the 69th New York Regiment

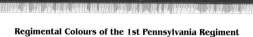

Stars and Stripes

per's Ferry (in Jefferson County, West Virginia). The Confederates considered this village as strategic, since it was at the confluence of the Potomac and the Shenandoah, and situated on the border of Maryland, Virginia and West Virginia; Johnston himself thought that the town had become indefensible and opted for withdrawing to Bunker's Hill some eighteen or so miles away.

Patterson at first refused to pursue him, fearing it was a trap. He was certainly in favour of a war of movement but was always frightened of falling into a trap and wondering also all the time what Washington was expecting of him. Finally he decided to cross the Potomac, believing that in the long term it was in the Manassas Plain that he would be able to beat General Johnston's troops most easily.

As far as cavalry was concerned, Johnston could count on James Ewell Brown "Jeb" Stuart (1833-64), a young West Point Graduate and a light cavalry specialist. He caused the Unionists quite some concern. On 16 July elements from Stuart's forces, sent to face Patterson's forces, came into contact with the Union forces. They struck along the Shenandoah Valley to pin the Unionists down. Faced with this situation Patterson tried to get closer to Charlestown but also asked for reinforcements, especially as his men had come to the end of their mobilisation. Most of the Confederate army was about eighteen miles from his positions.

For the Confederates, the situation seemed howe-

ver to be rather difficult to fathom. Beauregard invited President Jefferson Davis (1808-89) to take strategic decisions urgently. On the contrary, Davis was waiting for the Union to move and thus reveal their plans, and then react as a result. Johnston's confederate troops joined Beauregard's; meanwhile intelligence missions were increased, through spies in Washington, to find out what the positions

43

and the strength of the enemy forces were. Among these spies was Rose O'Neal Greenhow (1817-64) who was intimate with several Northern politicians, and who between 9 and 16 July 1861 managed to get information about McDowell's plan to Beauregard.

The press revealed nothing about McDowell's intentions except, it seems, the *New York Tribune* in its 17 and 18 July 1861 editions, giving information concerning McDowell's plan which might have been useful to General Beauregard; but the spies would not have really taken much notice of such articles in the press. Nonetheless the information transmitted in coded messages to Beauregard reached him by courier, above all women [7]. Beauregard ended up by deciding to plan his operations, by adopting, according to his statements and his convictions, Napoleon's plans at Austerlitz.

Basically the overall situation showed the opposing forces all moving, trying to react to what their respective executive powers expected – Davis in Richmond and Lincoln in Washington – who both wanted a decisive change of situation. In the field, it was some 50 000 to 60 000 inexperienced men who were getting ready to fight one of the war's "test battles", without their leaders knowing or mas-

tering a situation which was evolving constantly by the process of overall movement of the forces present.

FORCED MARCHES AND THE ADVERSARIES' PRE-POSITIONS

"Joe" Johnston could particularly count on the 1st Virginia Brigade under Jackson who, during the Battle of the Bull Run, was to earn the legendary name of "Stonewall" because of his courage in facing danger, showing how unfailing upright he was in the operational command of his troops. And in particular he was dreaded because he was known for his cut-and-dried opinions concerning the enemy. He would have preferred not to take prisoners, which was exactly what he himself said in January 1861 in the case of Virginia being attacked. And until his death in May 1863, he supported a war of invasion leading his own men with iron discipline, tolerating no infringements of his orders, either from his soldiers or his officers. Loathing desertion he even had thirty of his own men executed in August 1862. His conduct at Bull Run was to ensure his reputation as an intrepid general.

On the other side, McDowell's Union troops, about 34 000 men, crossed the bridges over the Potomac in front of Washington. These barely war-har-

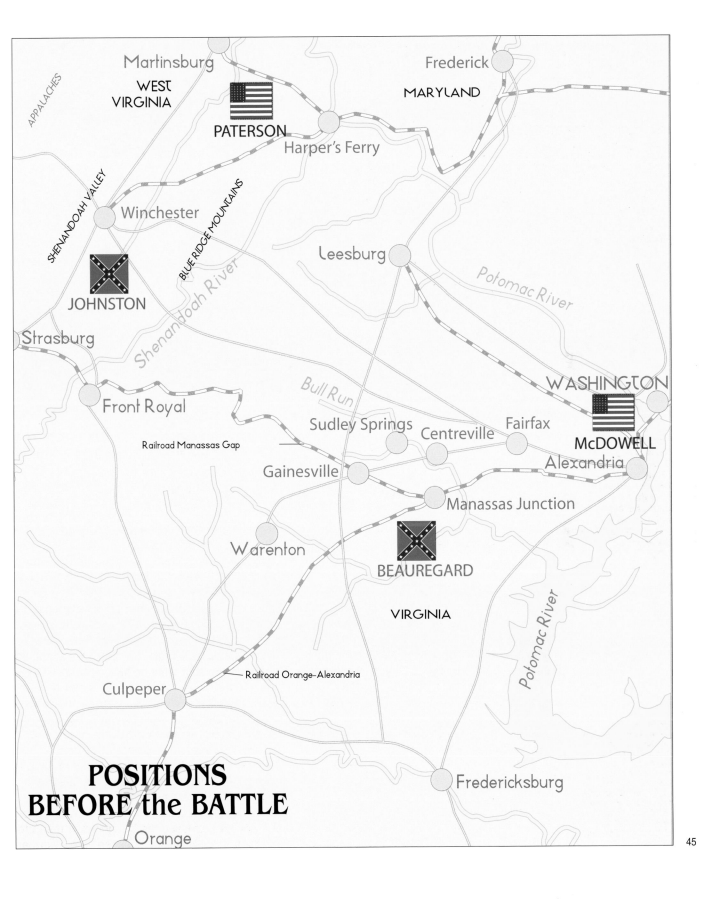

Martinsburg

WEST VIRGINIA

APPALACHES

PATERSON

Frederick

MARYLAND

Harper's Ferry

SHENANDOAH VALLEY

Winchester

BLUE RIDGE MOUNTAINS

Leesburg

Potomac River

JOHNSTON

Shenandoah River

Strasburg

Front Royal

Bull Run

WASHINGTON

Railroad Manassas Gap

Sudley Springs

Centreville

Fairfax

McDOWELL

Gainesville

Alexandria

Manassas Junction

Warenton

BEAUREGARD

VIRGINIA

Potomac River

Railroad Orange-Alexandria

Culpeper

POSITIONS
BEFORE the BATTLE

Orange

Fredericksburg

45

blistering heat.[8]

The men ended up standing under the sun, hanging around and becoming more and more unconcerned by their mission which was seen as becoming increasingly hazardous. Psychologically, this succession of setbacks got them down and the eager confidence they felt at the outset dwindled, giving way to a certain perplexity as to what was going to happen next.

Thinking that Johnston would not get to Beauregard before 20 July, if not the 21st, McDowell guessed he had four days to prepare for the battle. But his army was spread out along several miles and was not exactly quick. The Union columns stretched out in the sweltering July heat. The officers were at a loss at what to do with their soldiers who could not even keep serried ranks; they had to avoid coming across an enemy battery or dug-in position which would have broken up the column's advance once and for all; besides, because it was so big McDowell's army could not rely on any element of surprise. At the end of 16 July 1861, McDowell's troops reached Fairfax Court House where they set up camp. The men however showed clear signs of real physical exhaustion: they were not used to forced marches through the forests and across the fields.

On 17 July it was obvious that the Union troops could not progress more than eight miles; to this was added the almost total lack of discipline within the units, so much so that Virginian civilians were bullied and humiliated, as could only be done by columns of soldiers living off the country. The inhabitants of Fairfax Court House were even put to ransom, their houses looted and some burnt. The situation was similar for the people of Germantown where pigs were killed and children kidnapped.

The impression was of something a gigantic, multicoloured soldier's carnival, marching in their thousands, without any previous experience of such an occasion, convinced that they would soon be faced with an extraordinary situation.

Leading McDowell's column were four regiments (one from New Hampshire, two from Rhode Island and one from New York) all placed under the command of Colonel Ambrose E. Burnside and William Sprague, the young Governor of Rhode Island. It may seem surprising but at the beginning of the conflict it was thought natural for politicians to come directly onto the field to support the troops from

Above.
An infantry column moving along the valley of the Shenandoah, showing the forced march the Confederate troops had to make.
(RR)

Next Page.
During the battle while they advanced across the fields with fixed bayonets, as though detached from the harsh realities of life, the men stop to eat some blackberries growing profusely in the thick hedges.
(Composition by Ludovic Letrun, © Histoire & Collection 2010)

Opposite.
Infantryman from a Union infantry regiment wearing campaign dress at the beginning of the conflict. The kepi was very quickly preferred to the Hardee hat which was too heavy and cumbersome to go to war with. Moreover the kepi was much cheaper to produce than the regulation uniform hat.
(Private Collection, RR)

dened men advanced slowly, weighed down by the fifty pounds of gear on their backs, marching half as fast as experienced troops accustomed to forced marches.

In their race forward, the Union columns were frequently slowed down by the many trees the Confederates felled along their route. Orders were passed down the column and contributed to creating a concertina effect along the column in the

46

8. During this month of July 1861, the logbooks and the reports underlined the fact that the troops marched in the blistering heat.

their own state. The Unionists, starving and tired after a six-hour march, reacted with barely continuous salvoes to the Rebels' shooting.

Led by Brigadier-General Daniel Tyler (1799-1882) from the Connecticut Militia the army's vanguard, getting less and less determined, reached Centreville on 18 July; here, a few hours earlier, the Confederates were still solidly dug in with a network of trenches.

The Unionists, who had nothing to drink, searched for wells and water-tanks, filled up and set off again. They had to wait another day before the supplies officially organised for them caught up with them. Tyler then sent reconnaissance units to the Bull Run to try and estimate the Confederate forces. But the Yankees ran into Confederates at Blackburn's Ford and lost eight men.

Beauregard in fact disposed of 25 000 men, much better disciplined than the Unionists despite their summary equipment typical of irregular troops. The *Rebels* were spread out along eight or so miles of the Bull Run.

The advantage for the Southerners was that

Southern troops in place on the heights overlooking the battlefield of the Bull Run. (RR)

they had not had to use up all their strength on forced marches, unlike McDowell's Union troops.

McDowell, who had wanted to find out how dense the enemy lines were, saw how well dug in they indeed were, and on uneven terrain. He realised that he would have to abandon his initial plan of attack and decided to go round them by the north-west and go for an attack on the left flank. But he took an extra day to reach a decision for this new plan.

Meanwhile, the Confederates used the time they had to strengthen their position. Crowded trains brought in Johnston's men to Manassas, so that when McDowell launched his attack on the morning of 21 July, it was actually three Confederate brigades which had come up to reinforce the Southern lines; and a fourth was even on its way when the battle started.

Previous page, top left:
Leesburg Bridge, to the north of Alexandria, on the Potomac.
(RR)

Above, left:
A Confederate infantryman wearing full dress, posing for a studio photograph. The hunting horn was the insignia of the infantry and was not reserved just for the Chasseurs "à Pied" as it was in Europe.
(Private Collection, RR)

Above.
Confederate officers and soldiers posing in front of their bivouac on the eve of the battle.
(RR) 49

THE TIME FOR CONFLICT

BEAUREGARD HAD DISPOSED HIS TROOPS ON THE SOUTHERN BANK of the Bull Run River; it was lined with trees, to the north of Manassas. The railway line was also well guarded by the Confederates, as was the Warrenton turnpike bridge, six miles upstream and as were another dozen or so crossing points. At Warrenton the turnpike road coming down from Washington passed through Fairfax Court House and Centreville and meandered down the valley of the Bull Run, crossing the river over an arched stone bridge.

Below.
Before the battle, a Catholic priest says Mass for a Union regiment, no doubt made up mainly of Irish volunteers. Although this shot is taken after the battle, it does show this important moment before any engagement.
(RR)

The Unionists were convinced that the bridge was, if not heavily guarded by the Confederates, then at least mined. There was something else that worried the military leaders on both sides: the variety of uniforms the units were wearing. This raised a nagging question; once the battle started, wouldn't there be mistakes and confusion in all the turmoil? To avoid any misunderstandings that might have dire consequences McDo-well was relying on flags kept permanently unfurled to help the men pick out their insignia and the different neighbouring units. The Confederate troops seemed to be lacking in flags generally. By default, Beauregard was counting on pieces of cloth supplied by the Richmond womenfolk and intended to be worn on his men's shoulders as an identification sign. In the end it turned out to be a sort of rosette that the men wore on their jackets.

The toll bridge was only defended by 1 000 Confederates under the command of Colonel Nathan G. Evans. The artillery, reduced to its simplest expression, withstood repeated assaults by the Union infantry.

Letrun

51

(Composition by Ludovic Letrun. © Histoire & Collections 2010)

A SUNDAY FOR FIGHTING

At two in the morning on 21 July, McDowell's regiments moved and rushed along the Warrenton road, taking care to keep the campfires from the previous evening burning. McDowell had got his 10-000-strong column going to cover the six miles needed, through the brush growth and along the rutted paths. McDowell was thus counting on tricking the enemy into the real position of his forces. Units nonetheless remained at Centreville in reserve and watched their comrades going past, encouraging them to bring back souvenirs of the coming battles for them, a scalp here, a tunic button there, etc. The route taken went down towards the south-east of Centreville on to Manassas, passing through a series of fords – Mitchell's, Blackburn's, McClean's or Union Mills.

FIRST CLASHES AT THE BULL RUN TURNPIKE BRIDGE

Beauregard's troops were waiting steadfastly for the Unionists behind the Bull Run. Beauregard was expecting McDowell to attack the railway line, so much so that he placed nine brigades close by. McDowell was indeed counting on surprise to get hold of some of the

Southern positions but didn't want to hurry into the attack by rushing forward. He was waiting patiently for the reinforcements. He wanted however to position 14 000 men and reach, not the railroad as Beauregard thought, but the stone bridge over the Bull Run by making his men pass through the ford at Sudely Springs, by a circular movement on the right intended in the end to go round the Confederate army and surround it to a certain degree. The turnpike bridge itself was only defended by 1 100 Confederates, combining some infantry, a handful of cavalry and a little artillery under the command of Colonel Nathan G. Evans (1824-1868), from South Carolina, an inveterate drinker and nicknamed *"Shanks"* because of his long, spindly legs.

While McDowell's troops progressed from Centreville, part of whom was aiming to reach the left flank of the Southern forces, progressing 1,5 miles upstream of the Bull Run, regiments from Tyler's division advanced in the direction of the stone bridge and laun-

ched an attack which the Confederates were not expecting. It was already almost 11 a.m. Tyler had his cannon fire. From then on everybody knew that "contact" had been made.

Colonel Evans who was holding the bridge, saw the dust raised by the column in the main part of McDowell's forces; it convinced him that the attack against the bridge was only a feint. Little by little things started getting under way. Evans left four companies to watch over the stone bridge and regained the terrain to the north with his artillery. He was soon joined by a regiment from South Carolina and another from Loui-

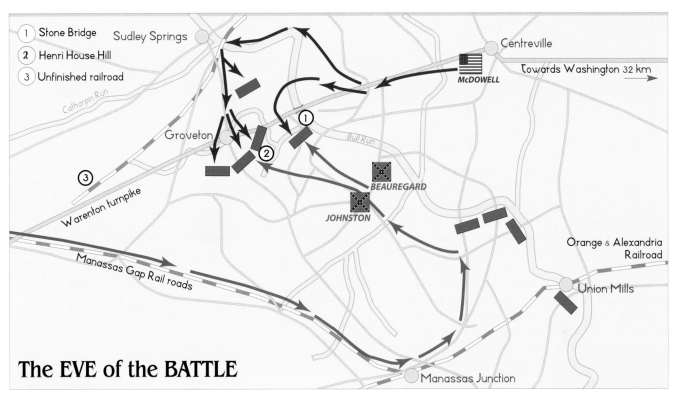

1 Stone Bridge
2 Henri House Hill
3 Unfinished railroad

Sudley Springs

Centreville

Towards Washington 32 km

McDOWELL

Catharpin Run

Groveton

Bull Run

BEAUREGARD

JOHNSTON

Warenton turnpike

Orange & Alexandria Railroad

Manassas Gap Rail roads

Union Mills

The EVE of the BATTLE

Manassas Junction

siana at the moment the Union column appeared on the hills. He sent part of his troops against the Yankees who were coming up across the fields. The Confederate troops fired and broke the Union rush. The Battle of Bull run had begun…

At his headquarters, Beauregard however thought that this clash was not really a major threat. It took the intervention of a staff officer, Engineer Captain Edward Porter Alexander, to bring the general back to reality. Alexander had in fact got close to Tyler's sector to see

Opposite.
General Tyler who started firing his cannon at 11 a.m.

Bernard Elliot Bee, Brigadier-General under General Johnston.

for himself if the Union columns were really there; his report had the effect of an electric shock.

Meanwhile, Evans' men were dangerously outnumbered, even though they had two artillery batteries. Facing them the Union soldiers were hardly more at ease since they feared Johnston's troops would arrive from the Shenandoah Valley. Evans and his men resisted as best they could but they were convinced that they needed reinforcements urgently. Finally it was a brigade from Johnston's army which arrived opportunely under the command of Brigadier-General Barnard Elliott Bee (1824-61) who was to die from a wound received on 21 July, with men from Mississippi, Alabama, and North Carolina; in all the equivalent of two brigades. Soon the Confederate artillery started bombarding the Union troops plentifully.

53

9. Wade Hampton commanded a legion he had himself partly financed. It comprised four cavalry companies, six infantry companies and an artillery battery.
10. Earlier he had confided to a friend that he was certain his end was near.
11. An officer commanding a Virginia battery on the confederate left flank, Captain Delaware Kemper was momentarily separated from his unit and fell right into the middle of a Yankee regiment. He was taken prisoner by a dozen infantry and insisted on surrendering his sword only to an officer; but like in the Southern ranks, overall organisation was inexistent and the Yankees did not know where to find a their officers. Finally through the woods, the group ran into some confederate soldiers who freed the unfortunate officer and got rid of his dozen guards.

McDowell's troops therefore increased the pressure they were putting on the Confederate positions which started to weaken. For two hours to the north of the turnpike bridge, 4 500 Confederates held off 10 000 Unionists but in the end they pulled back in good order at the price of fierce fighting. On both sides it was, for most of the soldiers, their baptism of fire. Inexperience took a great toll on the Union side, making it impossible for the officers to launch synchronized regimental attacks. The Confederates pulled back nonetheless, crossed the turnpike and reached a neighbouring hill, Henry House Hill, named after the Henry family who owned a farm on the crest. The line of the crest was soon the scene of terrible assaults on both sides.

When several regiments retreated to the rear precipitously, the Confederate lines were on the edge of breaking up. Those that remained in contact with the enemy were soon reinforced by the troops under Wade Hampton (1818-1902), from South Carolina [9] as well as by two regiments from Georgia, the 7th and 8th Georgia Regiments, led by Colonel Francis S. Bartow (1816-61).

On the crest line, the Southerners established a new front. It was now a matter of not giving in to the Union attacks which, from the north of the turnpike, threatened the whole Confederate flank to the west of the stone bridge. Johnston and Beauregard now clearly saw how decisively the situation was evolving, so much so that they moved units from the right flank to the left flank to reinforce it, towards Henry House Hill.

While the Confederate ranks were weakening under

Opposite, left.
The Confederate General Wade Hampton.
(RR)

Colonel Francis S. Bartow was at the head of the 7th and 8th Georgia Infantry Regiments.
(RR)

pressure from the Union and the regiments were moving back to the other side of the hill, in the middle of the day, Jackson's troops came to the rescue, in particular five Virginia regiments led by Brigadier-General Jackson. During their advance across the fields with fixed bayonets, as though detached from the harsh reality for a moment, the men found blackberries growing in abundance on the hedges and ate them.

When it came to the decisive moment of the confrontation, the troops on both sides were tired and relatively hungry. Most of them had lost their sense of direction and obviously had no idea of the tactical situation. The only thing that was certain for them was that the opposing lines were facing each other and that the soldiers had started firing salvoes, withdrawing several paces to reload before resuming their initial position and firing off another volley of lead.

The whole thing however was rather disorganised and very difficult for the officers commanding the troops. Evans, in the bridge zone, had a lot to do in this area. As for Bartow, he exhorted his men from Georgia to hold the position. But he was brutally killed by a bullet right in the heart on Henry House Hill just after changing his horse, his first horse having been killed. 1⁰

Thus for several hours during the afternoon of 21 July, attacks and counter-attacks, isolated or without coordination, followed one another on the slopes of Henry House Hill. Indeed this episode brought together a number of Civil War characters who more or less distinguished themselves subsequently. On the Northern side there was Ambrose E. Burnside (1824-81), Brigadier-General since May; William Tecumseh Sherman (1820-91) who became a byword for harshness; and Oliver O. Howard (1830-1909), each at the head of a brigade. Sherman, within Tyler's division, led the 3rd Brigade. Before this march on Manassas, Sherman had led several charges during the previous weeks in the sporadic and disorganised clashes along Warrenton Pike. The Battle of Bull Run however was in

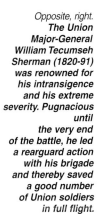

Opposite, right.
The Union Major-General William Tecumseh Sherman (1820-91) was renowned for his intransigence and his extreme severity. Pugnacious until the very end of the battle, he led a rearguard action with his brigade and thereby saved a good number of Union soldiers in full flight.
(RR)

General Oliver was like Sherman, at the head of a brigade at the Battle of the Bull Run.
(RR)

Below.
General Burnside at the head of a Rhode Island Infantry Brigade (1st and 2nd) and the 71st New York during the attack on the Confederate batteries.
(RR)

fact his real baptism of fire, at the head of very raw, quite inexperienced recruits.

On the Southern side, there were Beauregard and Johnston, the bold cavalry colonel, James E. B. "Jeb" Stuart; Wade Hampton who saw his South Carolina legion terribly torn to pieces during the battle; and Thomas J. Jackson, a former professor at the Virginia Military Institute, at the head of his brigade of Virginians.

Jackson, an austere, inspired Presbyterian saw everything through the distorting lens of his faith and considered the Yankees as Satan's fiends.

In the heart of the fighting, a shell exploded under Beauregard's horse, killing the animal outright, but leaving the general unscathed. Almost 6 000 Confederates were on the hill at that moment, in total disorder, so much so that half of them did not know exactly where their unit was. Only Barnard Bee's brigade and Wade Hampton's South Carolinas stayed in the line while the Unionists gained ground.

Disorganised units ¹¹ and inexperienced troops could be brought back under control by their officers on horseback who were there in their roles of guide, pointer and especially marker, both moral and psychological. Moreover from a didactic and directive point of view, the officers could be heard shouting and their boldness could become communicative. General Bee exhorted his men to regroup and rally the soldiers under

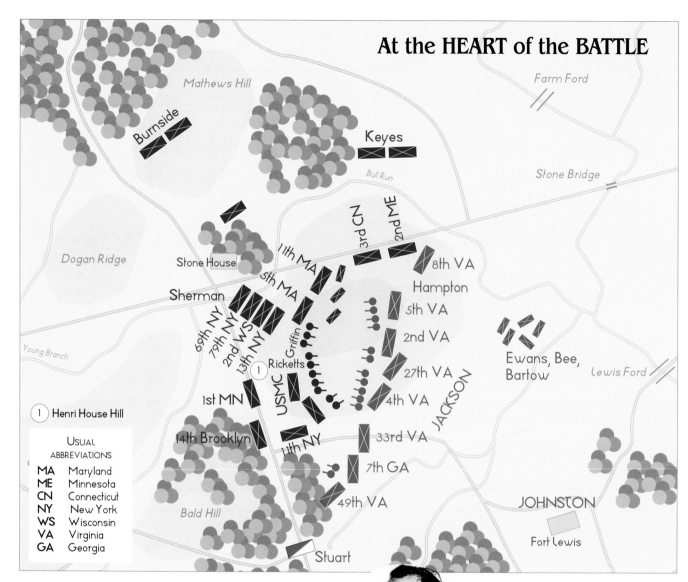

At the HEART of the BATTLE

Farm Ford

Mathews Hill

Burnside

Keyes

Bull Run

Stone Bridge

Dogan Ridge

Stone House

3rd CN

2nd ME

11th MA

5th MA

8th VA

Sherman

69th NY

79th NY

2nd WS

13th NY

Griffin

Ricketts

Hampton

5th VA

2nd VA

27th VA

Ewans, Bee, Bartow

Lewis Ford

Young Branch

JACKSON

4th VA

1st MN

USMC

33rd VA

14th Brooklyn

11th NY

7th GA

JOHNSTON

Bald Hill

49th VA

Fort Lewis

Stuart

① Henri House Hill

USUAL ABBREVIATIONS

MA	Maryland
ME	Minnesota
CN	Connecticut
NY	New York
WS	Wisconsin
VA	Virginia
GA	Georgia

This photograph taken on 29 April 1910 shows the very spot where General Jackson was given the nickname of "Stonewall" by General Barnard Lee. Jackson (opposite) was also wounded on this same site.

General Jackson whom he compared to a stone wall — "Stonewall", a nickname which stuck [12] — without anybody actually knowing whether it was a compliment praising his courage or whether he was expressing a certain annoyance because, faced with a perilously unpredictable situation, he wasn't being given any orders to pass on to his troops. *"Look at Jackson standing over there like a damned stone wall!"* But Barnard Bee was unable to clarify what he had said since he was mortally wounded in the abdomen and fell heavily from his horse. Nonetheless Bee's men reached the front line shouting, mixed with Jackson's

12. Jackson wanted the nickname to be attributed to his brigade rather than to himself. This was only done after his death, by decision of the Confederate government.

brigade and brought their rifles to bear as well; the Union assault was stopped in its tracks.

Facing them, McDowell's forces were now spread out in four brigades. But their tentative assaults were not very motivated or decisive. They only engaged some rather disparate regiments without this having any strategic influence on the course of the battle. McDowell's officers suffered from a real inability to coordinate their common undertaking.

On 21 July in mid-afternoon, almost 18 000 Union soldiers had nonetheless crossed the river. But McDowell only had less than 10 000 of them to launch an assault on Henry House Hill, because he was cut off

At the heart
of the fighting,
a shell exploded under
Beauregard's horse,
killing the animal
outright but leaving
the general unscathed.

(Composition by Ludovic Letrun, © Histoire & Collections 2010)

Above.
On these two pictures taken from a period newspaper (left) and a sketch for a more ambitious work (right), it is easier to appreciate the terrible fury of the fighting at the beginning of the day between the Confederate and the Union troops.
(RR)

Below.
It was near the Robinsons' House situated right in the middle of the battlefield, that General Barnard Bee compared General T.J. Jackson to a wall in order to encourage his troops to counter-attack, thereby forging Jackson's legend, the "Stonewall".
(RR)

from the rest of his forces. General Daniel Tyler had been unable to lead an attack to get across the stone bridge although his men had crossed the rived at Sherman's ford so that there was nothing between him, the attacking column and the troops situated to the east of the Bull Run.

The air was full of black powder smoke in stifling heat. Shots, explosions, screams and shouts followed one another, in the long term exasperating the soldiers; they were nagged by thirst, stunned by all the din without the slightest idea how the battle was evolving.

To support the assault, McDowell had two batteries commanded by Captains J. B. Ricketts and Charles Griffin set up on some heights south of Henry House Hill. These batteries increased their devastating fire, causing large gaps in the Confederate ranks but they soon came under accurate fire from the Southern infantry. Some of the Rebels had choice positions inside the house itself belonging to the Henry family. Without any qualms the Union gunners

Above, from left to right.
The two Northern artillery officers McDowell set up on the heights to the south of Henry House Hill: Captains Ricketts and Charles Griffin. *(RR)*

Opposite.
The Battle of the Bull Run has often been immortalised by the Union troops being routed. Rumour and exhaustion played in favour of the South which was nonetheless unable to exploit its victory fully.
(Private Collection, RR)

hit back, aiming at the house to get them out of it.

They killed Judith Henry, 80, a bed-ridden invalid who had refused to move out in spite of everything: a shell exploded in her bedroom, killing her outright. What's more, Ellworth's Fire Zouaves and a battalion of sailors were sent to reinforce the Union gunners. The Zouaves were dispersed by a charge made by a Virginian cavalry regiment, under by "Jeb" Stuart. The detachment of sailors, most of whom had only seen three weeks' service, broke and ran just as soon they came under fire from the Confederates. In spite of their efforts the Yankee officers were unable to keep order among the sailors and Zouaves.

A SCATHING SOUTHERN DETERMINATION

REBEL POWER
BULL RUN, VA.—JULY 21, 1861

The course of the battle might have depended on how effectively and skilfully the Union field artillery was positioned. But the confusion with the uniforms [13] ended up by being fatal for those gunners. At eighty yards from the position's first cannon, a Confederate regiment, the 33rd Virginia

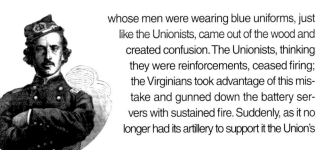

13. he flags could also be confused which is why Beauregard subsequently had the Confederate flag modified, with white stars on a blue St Andrews cross on a red background.

whose men were wearing blue uniforms, just like the Unionists, came out of the wood and created confusion. The Unionists, thinking they were reinforcements, ceased firing; the Virginians took advantage of this mistake and gunned down the battery servers with sustained fire. Suddenly, as it no longer had its artillery to support it the Union's

(Following on page 62)

Opposite.
Colonel Ellworth, commanding the New York Fire Zouaves. His troops did not particularly distinguish themselves on this tragic day.
(RR)

59

Burnside

Matthews
House

McDowell

Stone
House

Sherman

Porter

Ricketts

Runyon

Heintzelman

Jubal Early

Sherman

Ford

Stone Bridge

Robinson House

Tyler

worth

Henry House

Jackson

Beauregard

Jeb Stuart

Kirby Smith

Battle of First Bull Run (or Manassas)

July 21, 1861
Sunday, at the end of the day

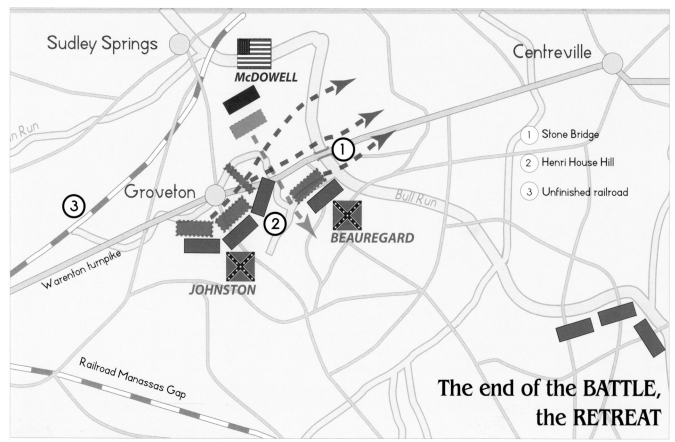

Sudley Springs

Centreville

McDOWELL

① Stone Bridge

② Henri House Hill

③ Unfinished railroad

Groveton

Bull Run

③

BEAUREGARD

JOHNSTON

Warenton turnpike

Railroad Manassas Gap

The end of the BATTLE, the RETREAT

(Continued from page 59)

infantry attack lost its drive and its cohesion. Meanwhile the potential strength of the Confederate forces reached its apogee with the arrival of two brigades at around 4 p.m.: those under Jubal Early (1816-94) from the right wing of Beauregard's army, and Edmund Kirby Smith's (1824-93) leading a brigade from Johnston's army.

Smith's brigade had barely got off the Shenandoah Valley train when it was indeed told to plunge into the fray. The general was seriously wounded there.

At the end of the afternoon, there were 18 000 men on hand on both sides. The Confederate troops were obviously less tired although the clashes had carried on for almost fourteen hours and the Yankees were starting seriously to feel the effects of the almost total lack of food and drink.

Now in Union hands, the Henry House was used by McDowell who set himself up on the top floor in order to get a better view of the battlefield. He saw his men trying to get across the plateau but the assaults broke up against the intense firing coming from the serried Confederate ranks. Attacks against both the Confederates' front line and their flanks like-wise failed.

Opposite.
With General Early's brigade (left), General Edmund Kirby Smith's cavalry brigade (right) played a decisive role in the last phase of the Battle of Manassas. Smith was seriously wounded in the melee.
(RR)

The Irish New York Volunteers go into the attack under the flag with the colours of green Erin. The embryo of the future Irish Brigade came to grips with reality for the first time in the Civil War.
(RR)

Above and opposite.
Two photos of the Sudley Methodist Church transformed into a Union hospital. Some Union medics remained with the wounded even though the Union troops were retreating and the Confederates were taking over the place.
(RR)

Early's and Smith's two brigades finished by destabilising the wing of the Union advance. As for Beauregard, he launched a counter-attack against Henry House Hill and wiped out the Union batteries.

From this moment onwards, the situation hustled on towards its inexorable conclusion. The Union army was seized by an uncontrollable urge to flee and there was nothing either McDowell or his officers could do to control it. The whole operation failed. Almost 12 000 Unionists let panic overcome them, wanting to survive after struggling for hours beyond their abilities; they had lost their regimental cohesion. The veterans' attitude was different from that of the young recruits. The veterans knew that tactical success and their survival depended on whether they could hold their ranks and positions. On the other hand, the inexperienced, undisciplined young recruits had all the trouble in the world staying in order, even more so in front of danger. They preferred seeking safety in dispersion and flight.

Once again, just like in a number of similar situations in military history, the psychological factor had its part to play. In this case, the Unionists were completely knocked off-balance, as has already been said, by their inability to seek out the enemy regiments' positions. But they were also frightened by the Rebel yell which was so distinctive and which cast real fear into the Union ranks, as a Union veteran recalled:

14. In James McPherson, op. cit. p 344

"There is nothing like it on this side of the infernal region. The peculiar corkscrew sensation that is sends down your backbone under these circumstances can never be told. You have to feel it." [14]

Paradoxically, the Confederate ranks were also close to being in the same situation panic-wise, so much so that participants and witnesses later wrote that when they saw the Confederate ranks beset by chaos and panic, they were convinced that the Confederates had been beaten. This was the impression that President Jefferson Davis indeed had when he himself reached Manassas from Richmond. A soldier at heart, he was eager to be in the heat of the action, and being unable to hang around in Richmond, he had taken a special train to Manassas, arriving on horseback with an aide de camp in the middle of the afternoon in the battlefield zone.

It was at headquarters that he learned that his army was within a stone's throw of winning. Discovering however that the ranks were wavering, proof in itself that nothing could really be taken for granted yet, he rallied the soldiers who were flowing back, shouting: *"I'm President Davis! Follow me to the battlefield!"* Apparently this had the desired effect and General Jackson, being tended for a wound to his hand in a field hospital near where the scene took place, got up and cried out: *"Give me 5 000 good men and tomorrow I'll be in Washington."*

This photo enables one to get an idea of the location of this First Battle of the Bull Run consisting mainly of rolling plains.
(RR)

65

Above:
Union troops going to the front. In a few hours, the retreat will have dispersed the participants and totally disorganised them. *(RR)*

Below.
Confederate infantryman wearing campaign dress. Note the blanket or the greatcoat rolled into a make-shift sheath made of guta percha, or waxed cloth, protecting it from the rain. *(RR)*

FROM A YANKEE RETREAT TO A YANKEE STAMPEDE

Given that all this was happening on a Sunday, a short while before the battle, a whole crowd of civilians from the capital's upper classes – a lot of Washington society women wearing the latest fashions, stiff and attentive, and dilettante officers without commands, and no fewer than six senators and at least ten members of the House of Representatives keen on the publicity and the opportunity to be right in the middle of a demagogic communication exercise, along with the curious and a few amateurs blinded by their thirst for a fight – all rushed towards the battle field.

A PICNIC ATMOSPHERE FOR THE WASHINGTON NOTABLES

This crowd was accompanied by some attentive journalists. Everybody passed through Centreville and reached a good position from which they would have a marvellous view of the battle. During the morning, a crowd of rubbernecks and onlookers rushed to the slopes between the Bull Run and the Cub Run stream, to the east of the battlefield. There was a picnic atmosphere, something extravagant and surrealist.

The onlookers were not taking any real risks since they were a mile and a half from the battlefield. Carriages and riders joined the mixed group standing, talking joyfully, eager for strong sensations. A few feminine laughs rang out nervously, their excitement badly concealed.

It seems in fact that all during the day this motley group of curious hardly saw anything of the fighting; they only heard infantry and artillery fire.

The battle zone was indeed covered by thick smoke and dust caused by gunpowder exploding as well as the troops moving along the main road. A lot of them did not know what fighting was really like and could not imagine for an instant the tragic turn events would take at the end of the afternoon, all the more so as regular reports were reaching them, even announcing that victory was imminent, good news which was immediately telegraphed to Washington.

A SHATTERING "RUN FOR YOUR LIFE"

The fact that the troops were in disorder and that a good number of Union soldiers were now separated from their officers ended by weighing heavily upon the day's outcome. In the stifling heat, most of them harassed by thirst, exhaustion and hunger, and above all not seeing any favourable outcome to the battle, the men let themselves to be overcome gradually by the urge to flee this deafening zone where everything was constantly hidden by gun smoke; to flee, find shelter, gather one's strength and above all drink.

In the end their thirst increased considerably because of the effect of dry air and gunpowder on the respiratory ducts which dried the mucous membranes and irritated the eyes.

Some tried to get away by floundering across the Bull Run, others fell back by Sudely Ford. This distraught retreat was nonetheless covered by a regular infantry regiment, supported by some cavalry and an artillery battery - a rearguard disposition on which the Confederates did not however really put undue pressure. But as the afternoon wore on, the number of runaways only increased under the startled gaze of the Washington onlookers, whose bucolic picnic atmosphere was giving way to the apprehension of a nightmarish end of afternoon to come.

Dozens of men, with or without weapons, followed each other. Then in the midst of frantic stampedes the numbers started swelling irremediably. Soon wagons mingled with the infantrymen; artillery batteries and caissons drawn by nervous teams became more and more frequent, making clouds of smoke and dust, in a din of hooves and wagon wheels.

Seeing the Union lines beginning to crumble away and fall back, the excited Confederates felt that victory was near and increased their barrage of infantry and especially artillery fire aimed at the stone bridge. A bull's eye destroyed a wagon on a little bridge over the Cub Run, thereby blocking the troops moving along this main and only escape route aside from the neighbouring fields and woods. As a result the runaways who had succeeded in crossing the bridge were sure to reach Centreville, unlike their unlucky comrades who were left stranded on the other side of the bridge.

They quickly clustered together in an indescribable throng of men and horses, amidst wagons, ambulances, and cannon, joined by increasingly terrorised civilians, especially the women who started screaming. Finally everybody started scarpering, running in all directions. Most wagons were abandoned, as were the ambulances and the wounded in them waiting to be evacuated to the hospitals. To all this was added the rumour that the Confederate cavalry was about to arrive and would most likely cut the runaways to pieces; they got rid of anything they could – rifles, backpacks – so that they could run away faster. Sherman with his brigade nonetheless succeeded in providing some sort of rearguard cover and in slowing down the Confederate's advance, thereby saving a good number of Union soldiers from capture or death.

Albert Riddle, a member of the Union Congress, with some others tried to stop the stampede, calling out to the Union soldiers. It was all in vain: *"the further they ran, the more frightened they grew […] we tried to tell them there was no danger, called them to stop, implored them to stand. We called them cowards […] we put out our revolvers and threatened to shoot them, but all in vain; a cruel, crazy, mad, hopeless panic possessed them, and communicated to everybody about in front and rear. The heat was awful, although now about six; the men were exhausted – their mouths gaped, their lips cracked and blackened with the powder of the cartridges they had bitten off in the battle, their eyes starting in frenzy; no mortal ever saw such a mass of ghastly wretches."* [15]

The Union soldiers' retreat changed very quickly into a real stampede and into indescribable

---

15 Quoted in Samuel S. Cox: *Three Decades of Federal legislation 1855-85*, Providence Publishers, 1885, p. 158, and quoted in James McPherson, op. cit. p. 345.

Below.
Union Zouaves forming a firing line under the orders of the company commander, on the left of the photograph. Note how very similar the volunteers' uniforms are to those of French North African troops of the same period. This shot was taken most likely during an exercise.
(RR)

chaos, a run for your life greeted by the shouts of joy from the Confederate soldiers who took hundreds of prisoners, especially when night fell, thanks especially to the Confederate cavalry squadrons who reached Bull Run and took a huge number of prisoners, including a Congressman who was immediately sent to Richmond under escort. Above all, the confederates seized materiel and ammunition, horses and carriages which were particularly welcome.

Meanwhile, McDowell took care to position the regiment under Colonel Louis Blenker (1812-63) – the 8th New York Volunteer Infantry.

Regiment (Miles' Brigade) from the 5th Division – in such a manner that it would cover the bridge and prevent the Confederates charging from this direction. He also bore in mind that he could consolidate his position on Centreville, 3 miles from the bridge. With this in mind he also kept the 5 000 men under Brigadier-General Theodore Runyon (1822-96) (4th Division of the North-Eastern Virginia Army) on some heights to the east of Centreville with twenty cannon and the battalion of regulars under George Sykes (1822-80).

McDowell was counting on holding Centreville so that the troops who were still on hand and falling back could rally his forces and reverse the situation. He even consulted Washington by telegram at the end of the afternoon towards 6 p.m. But his confidence contrasted greatly with his subordinates' state of mind. Indeed the men were all demoralised and the officers were quite incapable of influencing the demoralised troops.

There was no hope of rebuilding a front line on that side of the Potomac. There was nothing left to do but fall back again towards Arlington and hold the bridges over the Potomac. McClellan, who for a moment had been ordered to leave the Virginia

The inhabitants of Washington who had come "to watch the military parade" fled as totally panic-stricken as can be imagined. The courage and cool-headedness of the Confederate troops and their generals got the better of the Union's optimism.

The rout
of the Union troops
has been perfectly
immortalised by this
headlong flight
of the caissons
and the front limbers
of the Union
Artillery, the last
troops in theory
to flee a battlefield.
(The Capture of
Rickett's Battery
Sidney King, Private
Collection, RR)

Above, left.
In the background, the Sudley Methodist Church that was transformed into a Union hospital during the battle, overlooking the vestiges of the Sudley Sulphur Springs.
(RR)

Above right.
Several graves belonging to Union soldiers, hastily buried in a ditch, below the heights. (RR)

Opposite,
from top to bottom.
The day after the battle, the remains of the toll bridge.
(RR)

Next page.
The first exchanges of fire caused the first Confederate deaths, like here on Matthew Hill.
(RR)

The body of a Union infantryman after the battle. (RR)

A railway bridge destroyed at the exit of Centreville. (RR)

Top right.
A group of troopers at Sudely Ford, near the remains of the Sudely Sulphur Springs, in front of some children, a long time after the fury of the fighting…
(RR)

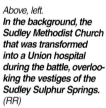

mountains and return urgently to the Shenandoah Valley, was finally ordered to stay put and wait for reinforcements which were sent him from Ohio; these orders were countermanded yet again and he was asked to hand over his troops to his subordinates, notably General William Rosencrans, and to come to Washington urgently.

Panic even started reaching corridors of power in Washington such was the scale of the disaster, to such an extent that the New York and Pennsylvania State authorities decided to send troops urgently.

To the south of the Bull Run, the Southerners continued taking prisoners, happy with their total victory. Faced with a victory of such magnitude that the Confederates had not exactly been expecting, President Jefferson Davis met with Generals Beauregard and Johnston, to discuss with them if all the options caused by this favourable situation had been envisaged.

Already in terms of numbers, the Union losses were impressive. Beauregard's men had been able to take 1 300 prisoners, capture 28 cannon, 37 artillery ammunition caissons, weapons, equipment, harnesses and uniforms, blankets, hospital stores, knapsacks, wagons, ambulances, not counting a considerable quantity of rifle ammunition. The number of Yankee soldiers killed was estimated at 500.

But they had also to consider exploiting the victory properly, before the Union troops could counter-attack. At 11 p.m., President Davis, learning of the state of panic at Centreville from the intelligence services and beyond, ordered his

two victorious generals to carry on advancing. But this idea had to be rapidly abandoned. The Confederate general staff decided in the end to reconnoitre in strength, without really seeking to break through further with their armies; this subsequently suggested that the Confederate leaders, Davis in particular, had wasted an opportunity to exploit the victory. The Confederate troops were in fact too disorganised to exploit the victory. This was the heart of a bitter controversy in the following weeks, with the Southern press castigating the military for not having grasped the opportunity to go and take Washington. Davis', Johnston's and Beauregard's partisans all blamed each other even though in July 1861 none of the main leaders thought it possible to capture the Union capital.

In the light of later military history and an analysis of the situation made by American historians, it seems almost certain that Johnston's forces would never have been able to reach Washington in less than 24 hours. On 21 July, McDowell was at Centreville to form a defensive line with his troops which had remained in reserve; he could count on more than 10 000 men who had not panicked, troops who would receive reinforcements to defend Washington and who were not at all ready to give in to an enemy force.

At best Johnston's troops might have occupied Centreville, but Johnston would have had to build fortifications to hold onto the Potomac region, especially for the winter, running the risk of a stalema-

Matthew B. Brady, the famous photographer to whom we owe most of the photographs of the Battle of the Bull Run. His reputation and his qualities as a reporter increased during the Civil War campaigns. (RR)

Bottom.
Pilgrimage or curiosity: the civilians, inhabitants of Washington return to the scene of the battle... and their frantic flight. This shot was taken at the foot of the monument commemorating the battle several years after the conflict. (RR)

troops reinforcing Georgetown, Arlington and Alexandria, apart from Centreville which held fast; and also especially because of the Confederate army's logistics shortcomings, even though General Patterson was convinced that he could reach Washington with his army, in spit of the fact that he would have had to cross the Potomac.

Early on the morning of 22 July, rain came to perfect the wretched picture of the Union troops' rout – a procession of dismembered units, with pitiful thirsty, hungry faces returning to Washington along roads now transformed into quagmires. These were demoralised, exhausted men who passed through Washington. Many sat on the stoops of houses; others fell asleep in spite of the rain.

So many rumours were flying around the Union Capital that some of the political elite thought that Washington was bound to be captured because everybody was expecting a Confederate offensive which would overwhelm everything because there was no defence. Nonetheless in less than twenty-four hours fresh and ready regiments had been rounded up and put into the line at Arlington to protect the Union capital.

Below.
The railway lines being rebuilt near Centreville.
(RR)

te and a war of position which was just as risky as it was unpredictable. And if the Confederates weren't able to reach the Union capital, the reason for this, as Johnston explained to Davis in the autumn of 1861, was because of the concentration of Union

TIME TO ASSESS

A lot has obviously been written about the Battle of Manassas – Bull Run and its consequences, which still deeply interest American historians. As in many like situations, the way the battle developed depended a lot on the troops' behaviour, their state of mind and the quality of their leaders.

In the Union ranks, it appears that a number of senior and junior officers, especially the ranks from lieutenant to major, were not cool-headed enough. Their nervousness and fear of being wounded or even killed predisposed the rank and file who, as is well known, are very watchful of the quality of their officers. This fear was catching and troubled them; the uneasiness then spread among the ranks and changed gradually into panic.

Thus the defeat can be laid at the door of the officers who were incapable of leading their troops, a quarter of whom had never been under fire before. The result for the Union was 450 to 500 killed, more than 1 100 wounded and between 1 500 and 1 800 missing, mostly taken prisoner.

On the Confederate side, there were 400 killed, more than 1 500 wounded and 13 missing. But between and a quarter and a third of the Southern troops did not take part in this battle which was fought by men who did not know how to manoeuvre under fire because they hadn't been trained enough. The lack of discipline was common to both sides. According

to McDowell's report, it seems that the Southerners were on the whole more effective where defence was concerned and less likely to become disorganised than the Union ranks.

The particularly densely wooded zones favoured the Confederates, screening their positions and especially their artillery batteries. Afterwards, Union voices were raised, like that of the abolitionist Wendell Phillips (1811-84), calling for an operation to destroy all Virginia's forests. Such ideas were greeted with acclaim in the northern states and it was not rare to hear radicals echoing this and even calling for the Southern states to be annihilated.

Whatever, McDowell was profoundly affected by the defeat. A week later he wrote to President Lincoln, suggesting that as far as he was concerned the cause was lost. In the New York Tribune, his remarks left a taste of defeatism when he wrote: *"We did not distinguish ourselves"*, an attitude which was greatly reproved by Horace Greeley (1811-72), the owner of the newspaper who thought that these prematurely triumphal or defeatist papers had to cease. All

Above.
After the first battle of Manassas, the Confederate troops occupied the terrain... waiting for the second battle. The winners considerably reinforced the approaches to the battlefield, as can be seen on this photograph taken in the spring of 1862.
(RR)

75

Above.
After the end
of the war,
the American
government erected
a monument
commemorating both
battles. A full strength
infantry regiment
poses in front of it.
(RR)

the same Greeley, who was one of the founders of the Republican Party, did hold particularly strong convictions where the Confederacy was concerned.

In the days following the battle, the government in Washington waited and Lincoln's entourage paid particular attention to rumours.

One of these, reported to the President directly, told of the capture of Arlington by the Confederates and of their imminent arrival in the capital. This was immediately denied by General Winfield Scott who exploded, saying: *"We now have some knowledge of what war can teach us and we have learnt what panic is. We must now be ready for all forms of rumour. So why, Mr President, should we believe for a moment that President Jefferson Davis has crossed Long Bridge at the head of a brigade of elephants and that he's crushing the citizens under foot? He does not have a brigade of elephants and in no case can he have one!"* Lincoln therefore took the time to decide and set about planning with methodical preparation how the war was going to be pursued, without excessive haste but with renewed governmental vigour.

For Sherman, the lessons he gleaned from Bull Run were clear: they had to rely more on training and disciplining the soldiers for the campaigns to come. For him the preparations had to be longer and there had to be enough money.

But defeatism did not spread to the Union for all that; the defeat at Bull Run, even if unacceptable, only encouraged them in their determination to give themselves the means to struggle and to persevere in the fight against the South; they also realised what the conflict and the trials to come would be like. Thus the first measures aimed to get the troops beaten at Bull Run back in hand, to reconstitute the units and to ensure that the men were supplied with food and water from a series of depots set up for the purpose.

In the four days following the battle, Lincoln wrote down what he considered was essential for the planning to come – directives aimed especially at reinforcing the blockade, creating a solid reserve of volunteers at Fort Monroe [16] which protected the port in Chesapeake Bay in Virginia, under the command of General Benjamin Franklin Butler (1818-93).

This contributed to the fact that during the whole war, the Union was able to use this port from which it could launch naval expeditions and ensure that land units could be transported. Lincoln also relied on Major-General John Charles Fremont (1813-90) for the operations on the Western front. Finally he suggested leaving Manassas Junction and Strasburg in enemy hands, but keeping the line open between Harper's Ferry and Strasburg. He envisaged a move from Cairo to Memphis and from Cincinnati to East Tennessee. Finally Lincoln called for efforts to be concentrated on the next large-scale operation against Virginia and for the blockade to be stepped up, particularly in Maryland. This was combined with Patterson being replaced by Nathaniel P. Banks at the head of the Union armies.

If in absolute terms, it took more or less time to put these plans into effect, from then onwards Washington nonetheless cautiously started putting together various operations and above all making sure the troops were well prepared and well supplied following on from the disastrous Battle of Bull Run.

On 22 July 1861, Lincoln signed the project for a law recruiting 500 000 men over three years. On 25 July he signed another project providing for a further 500 000 men to be recruited. Volunteers flocked in and several regiments reached the Washington outskirts to join training camps placed under the command of General George B. McClellan. Thanks to his professionalism, discipline was instilled into the units of volunteers who little by little were changed into real soldiers, under the command of good officers, the incompetent ones having been weeded out. These regiments assembled on the banks of the Potomac were to constitute the Army of the Potomac whose qualities in combat subsequently became famous. Nonetheless the impact of Bull Run was noticeable for a long time afterwards. McClellan always hesitated before committing large masses of troops for fear of running into a stronger adversary that a lot of officers and troops also dreaded, especially those who had been at Bull Run for whom the battle echoed more or less like a traumatism.

In terms of command, the idea of electing one's own officers had shown how limited it was because

16 Created originally by the English Captain John Smith whose name was linked to that of Pocahontas, in 1609, the fort was called Fort Algernoume at the time; then Fort George was built on the site which then became Fort Monroe at the beginning of the 19th century as a tribute to President James Monroe.
17. There was the same approach during the fighting in the Vendée in France after the Revolution where the peasants who had rebelled returned home to their trade before Galerne's incursion once the fighting was over.

76

some of them really revealed how inept they were; many of them were convinced that skills could be acquired quickly from experience on the battlefield. Besides, at Bull Run, this was revealed in the movement of panic among several officers which so disconcerted their units, a phenomenon which was all the more devastating in that in the various units and on the terrain, each soldier only had a fragmentary and muddled glimpse of the overall reality of the battle, to such a degree that the slightest rumour, the slightest hesitation or withdrawal can start conveying notions of disaster, leading to death. The instinct for survival, not understanding the situation, not knowing what the enemy was doing, all these encouraged them to imagine the worst and drove them to flee. The more competent officers and NCOs in the regular army had stood in the rear with the same type of forces along the border between the North and the South.

Too many officers were incriminated in the defeat at Bull Run, and on 22 July 1861, the Union Congress agreed to the setting up of Courts Martial to examine the files of the officers concerned in order to decide whether they were to stay in the army or not, to judge their qualities and decide if they were competent or not. In the following months hundreds of officers chose to resign or were invited to do so, though the idea of electing officers did not disappear from the Union forces, the principal of electing regimental commanders not vanishing before 1863. Among the Confederates, the practice lasted longer but concerned candidates who were already experienced and better qualified militarily since the Southerners had benefited from the skills of some 313 Union officers who joined their cause.

In Richmond in any case, the victory was greeted with truly popular delight. Church bells rang out and the Congressmen thanked God, believing He had given them victory, and proof of the their cause's legitimacy. Generals Johnston and Beauregard saluted the population of the South for their support and their "patriotic courage" and a large number of people were convinced that they had won a victory for their ideals.

General Beauregard nonetheless drew up a report made public in October in which he denounced a certain offhand manner on the part of President Jefferson Davis whom he reproached for taking his time before sending General Johnston's troops to reinforce his own forces, which almost resulted in total defeat.

Beauregard then proceeded to put himself forward, taking credit for the whole Battle of Manassas and taking advantage of the situation to revive the debate over the way the victory had not been not exploited which the press had criticised; he underlined that before Manassas, President Davis had indeed refused a plan of which Beauregard was the author and which foresaw just such a outcome. In fact Beauregard could not really accept the fact that he had been relegated to second-in-command to Johnston in Virginia. Davis was offended and made sure that he was moved on from Richmond and assigned in January 1862 to the Tennessee and Kentucky theatre of operations. The Confederates, far from giving up West Virginia, sent almost 20 000 men there in August 1861. But a good number of these men were still inexperienced soldiers recruited from the countryside, armed with smooth bore rifles, even sometimes with hunting rifles and worn out by mumps and measles.

To sum up, at the Battle of the Bull Run the North suffered a serious blow whereas the South became excessively confident and imprudent, even though the wounded returning to Richmond by night cast a chill over everybody because many realised naively that war and victory had a cost.

Davis noted that several Congressmen and even his Vice-President thought that the soldiers ought to be allowed to go home and resume their activities now that there was no operation of any importance planned. 1[7] Johnston told President Davis confidentially that he was worried by the fact that, in the end, the victory had actually totally disorganised his army: everybody, from the lowest officer to the lowliest private, thought he had done his duty and fulfilled his obligations towards his country and now thought of nothing else but having fun and delighting in the victory.

They would be cruelly disillusioned in the years to come…   ❐

THE FIRST, BUT NOT THE LAST

Uncontested tactical victory for the Confederacy, the Battle of Bull Run didn't end in 1861: there was another instalment, the following year during another major engagement from 28 to 30 August 1862.

This time the Virginia Army under the Union Major-General John Pope, reinforced by elements of the Army of the Potomac numbering more than 60 000 men confronted the Army of North Virginia under General Robert E. Lee with almost 55 000 men.

The First Battle of Bull Run delayed the Union's new attempt to invade Virginia by eight months; here again, after a series of battles with rather indifferent if not adverse results, the Union troops had to block the road leading to Washington. President Lincoln therefore immediately sent General Pope with orders to stop the Confederates' alarming advance at all costs.

General Pope therefore planned to reach Richmond, the Confederate capital. In July and August, the respective troop movements led to another major confrontation in the Manassas valley. The Union troops were again defeated and started a withdrawal they tried to make salutary. The Confederate troops wanted to crush them but were unable to do so at the very end of August and the beginning of September.

In the end the Union troops lost some 15 000 men against Lee's 9 000. But the figures were not really attested since, according to the sources, there were 400 Confederate dead and 1 600 wounded, against 625 Union killed or mortally wounded apart from 950 wounded and 1 000 prisoners. During this Second Battle of Manassas, the overall losses reached 25 000 killed taking into account the fact that 15% of the casualties died of their wounds.

General Pope's defeat contributed to his discredit and encouraged General Lee to take the war into the Northern states who realised how unwise it was for them to convince themselves too early that victory was theirs, and above all to anticipate a war which was turning out to be more arduous than imagined.

President Abraham Lincoln and his cabinet at the moment slavery was abolished, the founding act of modern and successful America.
(Private Collection, RR)

APPENDICES

CHRONOLOGY

1860

INDEX OF PROPER NAMES

ORDER OF BATTLE. CONFEDERATE FORCES

ARMY OF POTOMAC

Brigadier General P. G. T. Beauregard, Commanding
Colonel Thomas Jordan, Chief of Staff

● FIRST BRIGADE
Brigadier General Milledge L. Bonham
- **11th North Carolina.** Colonel William W. Kirkland
- **2nd South Carolina.** Colonel Joseph B. Kershaw
- **3rd South Carolina.** Colonel James H. Williams
- **7th South Carolina.** Colonel Thomas G. Bacon
- **8th South Carolina.** Colonel E. B. C. Cash
- **Alexandria (VA) Battery.** Captain Delaware Kemper
- **8th Louisiana.** Col Henry B. Kelly
- **1st Company, Richmond Howitzers.** Captain John C. Shields
- **30th Virginia Cavalry.** Colonel R. C. W. Radford
- **Munford's squadron.** Lieutenant-colonel Thomas T. Munford

● SECOND BRIGADE
Brigadier General Richard S. Ewell
- **5th Alabama.** Colonel Robert E. Rodes
- **6th Alabama.** Colonel John J. Seibels
- **6th Louisiana.** Colonel Isaac G. Seymour
- **1st Company, Washington Artillery.** Captain Thomas L. Rosser
- **Cavalry battalion.** Lieutenant-colonel William H. Jenifer

● THIRD BRIGADE
Brigadier General David R. Jones
- **17th Mississippi.** Colonel Winfield S. Featherston
- **18th Mississippi.** Colonel Erasmus R. Burt
- **5th South Carolina.** Colonel Micah Jenkins
- **Appomattox Rangers, 30th Virginia Cavalry.** Captain Joel W. Flood
- **2nd Company, Washington Artillery.** Captain Merritt B. Miller

● FOURTH BRIGADE
Brigadier General James Longstreet
- **5th North Carolina.** Lieutenant-colonel J. P. Jones
- **1st Virginia.** Major Frederick G. Skinner
- **11th Virginia.** Colonel Samuel Garland, J.-R.
- **17th Virginia.** Colonel Montgomery D. Corse
- **24th Virginia.** Colonel Peter Hairston J.-R.
- **3rd Company, Washington Artillery.** Lieutenant John J. Garnett
- **Amherst Rangers, 30th Virginia.** Captain Edgar Whitehead

● FIFTH BRIGADE
Colonel Philip St. George Cocke
- **8th Virginia.** Colonel Eppa Hunton
- **18th Virginia.** Colonel Robert E. Withers
- **19th Virginia.** Lieutenant-colonel John B. Strange
- **28th Virginia.** Colonel Robert T. Preston
- **49th Virginia (3 companies).** Colonel William "Extra Billy" Smith
- **Schaeffer's Virginia Battalion Infantry (3 companies).** Captain F. B. Schaeffer
- **Loudoun (VA) Battery.** Captain Arthur L. Rogers
- **Lynchburg Artillery.** Captain H. G. Latham
- **Wise Troop.** Captain John S. Langhorne
- **Franklin Rangers.** Captain G W H Hale
- **Bedford Southside Dragoons.** Captain J. Wilson

● SIXTH BRIGADE
Colonel Jubal A. Early
- **7th Louisiana.** Colonel Harry T. Hays
- **13th Mississippi.** Colonel William Barksdale
- **7th Virginia.** Colonel James L. Kemper
- **4th Company, Washington Artillery.** Lieutenant Charles W. Sq

● EVANS' BRIGADE
Colonel Nathan G. Evans
- **1st Louisiana Battalion.** Major Chatham R. Wheat (wounded)
- **4th South Carolina.** Colonel J. B. E. Sloan
- **Campbell Rangers, 30th Virginia Cavalry.** Captain John D. Alexander
- **Clay Dragoons, 30th Virginia Cavalry.** Captain William R. Terry
- **Artillery Battery.** Lieutenant G. S. Davidson

● RESERVE BRIGADE
Brigadier General Theophilus H. Holmes
- **1st Arkansas.** Colonel James F. Fagan
- **2nd Tennessee.** Colonel William Bate
- **Purcell (VA) Artillery.** Captain R. Lindsay Walker
- **Hampton's SC Legion.** Colonel Wade Hampton III (wounded), then Captain James Conner
- **Camp Pickens Battery.** Captain Sterrett of the C.S. Navy

ARMY OF SHENANDOAH

Brigadier General Joseph E. Johnston, commanding

● FIRST BRIGADE
Brigadier General Thomas J. Jackson
- **2nd Virginia.** Colonel James W. Allen
- **4th Virginia.** Colonel James F. Preston
- **5th Virginia.** Colonel Kenton Harper
- **27th Virginia.** Ltc John Echols
- **33rd Virginia.** Colonel Arthur C. Cummings
- **Rockbridge Artillery.** Captain John P. Brockenbrough

● SECOND BRIGADE
Colonel Francis S. Bartow (killed), then colonel Lucius J. Gartrell
- **7th Georgia.** Colonel Lucius J. Gartrell
- **8th Georgia.** Lieutenant-colonel William M. Gardner (wounded)
- **Wise Artillery.** Captain E. G. Alburtis, Lt John Pelham

● THIRD BRIGADE
Brigadier General Barnard Elliott Bee, J.-R. (killed), then colonel States Rights Gist
- **4th Alabama.** Colonel Egbert Jones (killed)
- **2nd Mississippi.** Colonel William Clark Falkner
- **11th Mississippi (companies A & F).** Ltc Philip F. Liddell
- **6th North Carolina.** Colonel Charles F. Fisher (killed)
- **Staunton Artillery.** Captain John Imboden

● FOURTH BRIGADE
Brigadier General Edmund Kirby Smith (wounded), then colonel Arnold Elzey
- **1st Maryland Battalion.** Lieutenant-colonel George H. Stuart
- **3rd Tennessee.** Colonel John C. Vaughn
- **10th Virginia.** Colonel Simeon B. Gibbons
- **13th Virginia.** Colonel A. P. Hill
- **Culpeper Artillery.** Lieutenant Robert F. Beckham

● ARTILLERY
- **Pendleton's Battery.** Captain William N. Pendleton
- **Thomas Artillery.** Captain P. B. Stanard

● CAVALRY
- **1st Virginia.** Colonel J. E. B. Stuart

ORDER OF BATTLE. UNION FORCES

Brigadier General Irvin McDowell, commanding in chief

ARMY OF NORTHEASTERN VIRGINIA

Brigadier General Irvin McDowell, commanding
Major William Farquhar Barry, artillery commander

FIRST DIVISION
Brigadier General Daniel Tyler

● **FIRST BRIGADE**
Colonel Erasmus D. Keyes
- **2nd Maine.** Colonel Charles D. Jameson
- **1st Connecticut.** Lieutenant John Speidel
- **2nd Connecticut.** Colonel Alfred H. Terry
- **3rd Connecticut.** Colonel John L. Chatfield

● **SECOND BRIGADE**
Brigadier General Robert C. Schenck
- **2nd New York.** Colonel George W. B. Tompkins
- **1st Ohio.** Colonel Alexander M. McCook
- **2nd Ohio.** Lieutenant Rodney Mason
- **Company "E", 2nd US Artillery.** Captain James Howard Carlisle

● **THIRD BRIGADE**
Colonel William T. Sherman
- **13th New York.** Colonel Isaac F. Quinby
- **69th New York.** Colonel Michael Corcoran (wounded and captured), captain James Kelly
- **79th New York.** Colonel James Cameron
- **2nd Wisconsin Volunteer Infantry Regiment.** Lieutenant-colonel Henry W. Peck, colonel S. Park Coon
- **Company "E", 3rd US Artillery.** Cpt Romeyn B. Ayres

● **FORTH BRIGADE**
Colonel Israel B. Richardson
- **1st Massachusetts.** Colonel Robert Cowdin
- **12th New York.** Colonel Ezra L. Walrath
- **2nd Michigan.** Major Adolphus W. Williams
- **3rd Michigan.** Colonel Daniel McConnell, lieutenant-colonel Ambrose A. Stevens
- **Company "G", 1st US Artillery** (2 guns). Lieutenant John Edwards, J.-R.
- **Company "M", 2nd US Artillery** (4 guns). Captain Henry J. Hunt

SECOND DIVISION
Brigadier General David Hunter (wounded), colonel Andrew Porter

● **FIRST BRIGADE**
Colonel Andrew Porter
- **8th New York Militia.** Col George Lyons
- **14th New York Militia (14th Brooklyn).** Colonel Alfred M. Wood (wounded), Lieutenant-colonel Edward Brush Fowler
- **27th New York.** Colonel Henry W. Slocum (wounded), major Joseph J. Bartlett
- **US Infantry Battalion** (8 companies). Maj George Sykes
- **US Marine Corps Battalion.** Major Joseph G. Reynolds
- **5th US Cavalry Battalion** (7 companies). Major Innis N. Palmer
- **Company "D©, 5th US Artillery.** Captain Charles Griffin

● **SECOND BRIGADE**
Colonel Ambrose Burnside
- **2nd New Hampshire.** Colonel Gilman Marston (wounded) Ltc Frank S. Fiske
- **1st Rhode Island.** Major Joseph P. Balch
- **2nd Rhode Island.** Colonel John S. Slocum (killed) then lieutenant-colonel Frank Wheaton and major Sullivan Ballou (killed)
- **71st New York.** Colonel Henry P. Martin
- **2nd Rhode Island Battery.** Cpt William H. Reynolds

THIRD DIVISION
Col Samuel P. Heintzelman (wounded)

● **FIRST BRIGADE**
Colonel William B. Franklin
- **5th Massachusetts.** Colonel Samuel C. Lawrence (wounded)
- **11th Massachusetts.** Colonel George Clark, Jr.
- **1st Minnesota.** Colonel Willis A. Gorman
- **4th Pennsylvania.** Colonel John F. Hartranft
- **Company "I", 1st US Artillery.** Captain James B. Ricketts (wounded and captured), lieutenant Edmund Kirby

● **SECOND BRIGADE**
Colonel Orlando B. Willcox (wounded and captured), colonel J. H. Hobart Ward
- **11th New York "First Fire Zouaves".** Lieutenant-colonel Noah L. Farnham (wounded)
- **38th New York.** Colonel J. H. Hobart Ward, Lieutenant-col. Addison Farnsworth
- **1st Michigan.** Major Alonzo F. Bidwell
- **4th Michigan.** Colonel Dwight A. Woodbury
- **Company "D", 2nd US Artillery.** Captain Richard Arnold

● **THIRD BRIGADE**
Colonel Oliver O. Howard
- **3rd Maine.** Maj Henry G. Staples
- **4th Maine.** Col Hiram G. Berry
- **5th Maine.** Col Mark H. Dunnell
- **2nd Vermont.** Col Henry Whiting

FORTH DIVISION
Brigadier General Theodore Runyon

● **MILITIA**
- **1st New Jersey.** Colonel Adolphus J. Johnson
- **2nd New Jersey.** Colonel Henry M. Baker
- **3rd New Jersey.** Colonel William Napton
- **4th New Jersey.** Colonel Matthew Miller, Jr.
- **Volunteers. 1st New Jersey.** Colonel William R. Montgomery
- **2nd New Jersey.** Colonel George W. McLean
- **3rd New Jersey.** Colonel George W. Taylor
- **4th New Jersey.** Colonel (?)
- **41st New York.** Colonel Leopold von Gilsa

FIFTH DIVISION
Colonel Dixon S. Miles

● **FIRST BRIGADE**
Colonel Louis Blenker
- **8th New York.** Ltc Julius Stahel
- **29th New York.** Col Adolph von Steinwehr
- **39th New York.** Col Frederick G. D'Utassy
- **27th Pennsylvania.** Col Max Epstein
- **Company "A", 2nd US Artillery.** Captain John C. Tidball
- **8th New York Militia Battery.** Captain Charles Brookwood

● **SECOND BRIGADE**
Colonel Thomas A. Davies
- **16th New York.** Ltc Samuel Marsh
- **18th New York.** Colonel William A. Jackson
- **31st New York.** Colonel Calvin E. Pratt
- **32nd New York.** Colonel Roderick N. Matheson
- **Company "G", 2nd US Artillery.** Lieutenant Oliver D. Greene

81

BIBLIOGRAPHY

— *The Coming Fury. Vol. one. The Centennial History of the Civil War.* Bruce Catton, *Doubleday & Company, Inc.* New York, 1961, 565 pages.

— *Terrible Swift Sword. Vol. two. The Centennial History of the Civil War.* Bruce Catton, *Doubleday & Company, Inc.* New York, 1963, 559 pages.

— *The Destructive War. William Tecumseh Sherman, Stonewall Jack son and the Americans.* Charles Royster, *Editions Alfred A. Knopf,* New York 1991, 523 pages.

— *The Blue and The Gray. The Story of the civil war as told by participants.* Henry Steele Commager (ed.), *The Bobbs-Merrill Company, inc.,* new York, 1950, 1201 pages.

— *Battle at Bull Run: A History of the First Major Campaign of the Civil War.* William C. Davis, *Stackpole Books,* second print, 1995, 336 pages.

— *Civil War Harper's Weekly* du 3 août 1861.

— *The South was right.* James Ronald Kennedy, Walter Donald Kennedy, *Pelican Publishing Company,* Gretna, 1997, 431 pages.

— *Battle Cry of Freedom. The Civil War Era.* Editions Oxford University Press, 909 pages.

The author thanks Laurent Fournier for his precious help.

Cover: The Capture of Rickett's Battery, Sidney King, private collection, RR; illustration by Ludovic Letrun,
© Histoire & Collections 2010. Back Cover: Congress Library, RR and illustration by André Jouineau, © Histoire & Collections 2010

RR for Library of Congress, Washington, DOD (Department of Defence) and Private Collection.

This book has been realised by Jean-Marie Mongin
Histoire & Collections 2010

ISBN: 978-2-35250-153-4

Publisher's Number: 35250

a book printed by
HISTOIRE & COLLECTIONS
5, avenue de la République
F-75541 Paris Cédex 11

Fax 01 47 00 51 11
www.histoireetcollections.fr

This book has been designed, typed, laid-out and processed by *Histoire & Collections* and *"le Studio Graphique A & C"* on fully integrated computer equipment

Color separation: Studio A&C

Printed by Zure, Spain, EEC

October 2010